Rebecca

Rebecca

KINGDOM OF
CATS

National Wildlife Federation

Wherever I've been—the wilds of Idaho or the searing heat of an African plain—I have found that people love and fear, hate and revere, the cats of the world.

I recall the fear in the eyes of farmers in northern India, who refused to harvest a field of sugar cane because a tigress and her cubs had moved into that beautiful cover. The farm owner had to drive her away with his faithful elephant.

Similar fear showed in the house-boy in Africa's Serengeti, who burst into the room, his eyes wide with fright. "Bwana—simba!" he hissed. Flashing a powerful light from the back door, we sighted a huge lioness, her face and jaws covered with the blood of a Thomson's gazelle she had killed within 50 yards of the house.

Recognition and respect showed in the faces of two old farmers in northeast China when we approached them to inquire about the presence of tigers. Shy, they said. Not here anymore but over the ridge, they said, gesturing toward Siberia. But leopards, yes. Just the day before, they had witnessed a leopard kill a pig in their field. They liked the leopard because it killed the wild pigs that rooted up their potatoes.

I was the first American they had seen and they asked why I was interested in tigers. To learn about them, my interpreter informed them. Good luck, they mused, and in diplomatic silence, returned to their plowing.

Grim determination best describes the attitude of the park wardens patrolling for jaguar poachers in the spectacular Iguazu Park, straddling the borders of Argentina, Brazil, and Paraguay. The jaguar has been hunted relentlessly. It survives, but as the forest disappears, so will the jaguar.

The American mountain lion, my special cat, has literally avoided man's efforts to annihilate it. True, we did manage to remove the cougar from many of our 50 states, but it doggedly held on in the remaining wilderness and rimrocks of the West (a remnant population still survives in Florida). The cougar's stealth, brains, and secretive lifestyle have kept him from the fate of the wolf. Today, because of new knowledge and an enlightened public, the cougar is doing well in most of its range.

The big cats awe and impress us, but the small ones also elicit a variety of human emotions. From those who are valued for their fur, such as our American lynx and bobcat, to those who simply capture our imagination, such as the Asian fishing cat, humans view them with feelings ranging from greed to admiration.

Yet we still know so little about most of the world's wild cats. Because they are so secretive, solitary, and largely nocturnal, and because some of them inhabit harsh environments, they are difficult to study.

As the world's human population grows and alters irreversibly many environments, we may lose some species before we learn anything about them. One third of the world's 37 species of cats are considered threatened, if not endangered.

I hope this book will help increase our appreciation of the world's cats and perhaps help bring about a plan to save them. Then generations to come can enjoy the beauty, strength, and mystery of all the world's cats.

— Maurice Hornocker

A pioneer in his field, Maurice Hornocker is now the dean of cougar researchers. But back in 1963, he was just a young biologist trying to study cougars in the wild by capturing, tagging, and then recapturing them. Radio telemetry had not yet been refined, and the years Hornocker spent in the mountains were ground-breaking work in learning about cougar behavior—and in changing public opinion about the big cats. He later did research on leopards, bobcats, and lynx, and now is director of the Wildlife Research Institute at the University of Idaho and a scientific consultant to the National Wildlife Federation.

KINGDOM OF
CATS

NATIONAL WILDLIFE FEDERATION

CONTENTS

NATURE OF CATS

by Fiona Sunquist

Library of Congress
Cataloging in Publication Data

Kingdom of cats.

Includes index.
Contents: Nature of cats / by Fiona Sunquist — North America / by Gary Turbak — Latin America / by Fiona Sunquist — (etc.)
1. Felidae.
I. National Wildlife Federation.

QL737.C23K56   1987   599.74'428
87-20226
ISBN 0-912186-84-4

NORTH AMERICA

by Gary Turbak

LATIN AMERICA

by Fiona Sunquist

ASIA AND EUROPE

by Peter Jackson

AFRICA

by Norman Myers

CATS IN OUR LIVES

by Elaine S. Furlow

The five photographs on the next pages capture many qualities of the world's cats—their beauty, power, grace, strength, and even their tenderness toward a cub.

First overleaf: Leopard stalking prey, Wankie National Park, Zimbabwe, Africa

Second overleaf: Tiger running, Ranthambhore, India

Third overleaf: Lynx exploring with her kitten, western Montana

Fourth overleaf: Jaguar resting in a tree, Mato Grosso, Brazil

Fifth overleaf: Lion bringing down a wildebeest, Masai Mara, Africa

A leopard roams the rain forests of Africa, while a secretive lynx haunts snow-covered mountains in Montana. Their size and habitat may vary, yet the world's cats still are astonishingly alike—an enchanting combination of beauty and utility. What are cats like? At any given moment, they are mysterious, graceful, powerful, a bit elusive and aloof. This book celebrates feline beauty, strength and stealth—the wondrous qualities of the world's cats.

THE NATURE OF CATS

This domestic cat's sensitive whiskers attest to its heritage of life among dim shadows. Whiskers help domestic and wild cats alike maneuver their way through underbrush.

BY FIONA SUNQUIST

The members of some animal families don't resemble each other at all. The minute Chihuahua and the massive St. Bernard, for instance, might be different species for all they resemble each other. Cats, on the other hand, are instantly recognizable as cats, no matter what their size, no matter where they are found. A four-pound black-footed cat, among the smallest of cat species, looks like a scaled down version of its larger wild relatives; all felids, from the powerful tiger to the ordinary housecat, behave similarly.

When his voyage on the *Beagle* reached South America in 1833, scientist Charles Darwin observed three trees scratched by jaguars: "I imagine this habit of the jaguar is exactly similar to one . . . seen in the common cat, as with outstretched legs and claws it scrapes the leg of a chair."

An early observer of natural history, William Salmon, noted that "cats are Beasts of Prey, even the tame ones." He was right. Wild cats bring together movement and muscles, eyes and teeth, coloration and claws to make them effective predators. As behaviorist Konrad Lorenz wrote, "There are certain things in Nature in which beauty and utility, artistic and technical perfection, combine in some incomprehensible way: the web of a spider, the wing of a dragon-fly, the superbly streamlined body of the porpoise, and the movements of a cat."

If you shine a flashlight on a cat at night, its eyes glow with an almost metallic yellow-green lustre. This eyeshine has been the ingredient of legend—witch hunters in the Middle Ages thought it sprang from the fires of Hell—but in reality, it is simply a result of the cat's eye structure and an adaptation for hunting in little light.

When light enters a human eye, the retina absorbs and uses some of it, but the rest is lost. Not so in the cat's eye. In darkness, its pupils expand until they seem to occupy the whole eye. The wide-open pupils let faint light pass through the iris and strike the

The pupils of the jaguarundi's eyes (left), like those of other cats, expand to take in more light when it's dark. Cells bounce light back from the retina, helping cats to see in dim light and also producing their legendary eyeshine.

tapetum lucidum, layers of reflecting cells. As it does in all carnivores, the *tapetum lucidum*, meaning "bright carpet," acts like a mirror, reflecting light back to the retina, in a sort of ping-pong effect. Thus a cat gets a second chance to use light that would have escaped and been lost as it is in the eye of a human. It is this reflecting light that we humans see as the cat's yellow-green eyeshine.

For cats, the device helps improve vision in the dark. Cats' vision at night is about six times better than that of humans. At night, cats can see in what to humans is pitch dark, thus improving their chances of finding prey.

Cats also have highly developed peripheral vision. When a domestic cat is not asleep, it seems to spend much of its time just gazing into space, a habit that probably contributes to the cat's reputation of being aloof and mysterious. However, the far-away look has more to do with the structure of the cat's eye than with anything we humans might label "personality." When a cat looks as if it is languidly dreaming, it can actually be watching everything.

When a cat *is* asleep, it runs through many short sleep cycles, waking up to check out a sound or a blur of movement, then going back to sleep if nothing interesting is going on (hence the term *cat nap*).

A cat's ears, too, are important for survival. They help it locate prey and escape harm. Some cats, such as the large-eared serval, rely on sound more than others, such as the cheetah, whose daytime hunting habits depend primarily on sight. Interestingly, humans can pinpoint the source of a sound better than housecats can.

In cats, as in humans, the outer ears funnel sound into the inner ears. The cat's inner ears monitor more than sound, however. They also help a cat orient itself so that it lands on its feet when it leaps from a perch. Much like a ballet dancer pirouetting, a cat uses its vision and the signals from its inner ears to keep its balance.

Like its domestic cousin (right), a cougar (below) carries her cub by gripping its neck fur between her teeth. The cub probably feels no pain due to the loose folds of its neck skin.

A cat's tongue feels like 50 grit sandpaper. It is so rough it can rasp meat from bone or lick hair off of a prey's skin. The tongue also serves as a grooming tool for both the domestic cat (right) and wild cats such as the cheetah (below right).

Along with messages from the ears and eyes, a superb reflex helps a falling cat to right itself. In an automatic twisting reaction, the head rotates, then the spine and rear quarters align. At the same time, the cat arches its back to reduce the force of the impact when all four legs touch ground.

A cat's sinuous movements and graceful jumping and climbing skills always delight the watcher. An exceptionally limber spine and strong muscles allow cats to flex and twist in amazing ways. Some cats, such as the margay and clouded leopard, can even climb down trees headfirst.

The cat's ability to move with ease and to freeze for long periods are also keys to successful hunting. Almost all the wild cats live in dense grass, brush, or jungle, and they must capture their prey within a short distance or it will escape. So they rely on stalking, hiding, and rushing to give them a better chance of surprising—and thus overwhelming—their prey. A cat can freeze motionless and hold the position for half an hour or more, if need be, until it can creep closer for the final dash.

Cats may climb into trees to rest or to cache prey; but, contrary to popular opinion, they don't ordinarily leap out of trees onto the backs of prey. Most cats bound toward the prey in a final rush and, with their hind feet firmly planted on the ground for stability and leverage, kill their victim with a sweeping blow from their front paws or a powerful bite

Most cats, like the lion
(below), boast long,
impressive canine teeth
to make a killing bite.
But to slice into the
meat, they use their
razor-like rear teeth.

A cat's canine teeth grip prey (left) in a vise. To shear off the prey's flesh, however, cats turn their heads sideways and use their back teeth, as this bobcat is doing (below).

to the prey's neck or throat. Behaviorist Paul Leyhausen observed that even when a cat does spring onto prey from above, the cat first jumps to the ground, *then* plants its hind feet and rears up in a final spring.

When cats use the lengthy stalk and ambush technique on a bird, the bird often escapes by flying away. Only a few cats, such as the jaguarundi and serval, break the cat's cardinal rule of capture. They leap high into the air with all four feet off the ground, swatting at the bird in mid-air.

To hook and hold ground prey, however, a cat uses the most potent weapons in its arsenal: claws and jaws.

All wild cats (except the cheetah, fishing cat, and flat-headed cat) have claws that completely retract into their paws. The phrase "retractable claws" makes it sound as if a cat pulls in its claws voluntarily, but it doesn't. In fact, the opposite happens. When a cat is resting, its claws are automatically retracted into fleshy sheaths. When a cat wants to snare prey, it quickly extends its claws.

Most cats kill small prey by biting them on the back of the neck. The cat's canine teeth punch like an awl between the prey's vertebrae, severing the spinal cord. The victim dies almost instantly. The tiny gap between the vertebrae is almost an impossibly small target, but a high concentration of nerves around the canine teeth allows the cat to "feel" for the right spot between the bones.

When lions and tigers attack large grazing animals, they often bite the throat rather than the neck. Large ungulates have thick slabs of shoulder and neck muscles, as well as dangerous antlers or horns. A throat bite does not kill them as fast as a neck bite does, but it is much safer for the cat. The prey generally suffocates to death.

The only cat without such powerful canine teeth is the cheetah. Cheetahs have small canines, perhaps—strange as it might sound—because they run so fast.

The canine teeth of tigers or leopards have large roots that take up much space in the nasal cavity. The cheetah, however, needs plenty of oxygen during its high speed chases. One theory is that the cheetah evolved larger nostrils for increased air intake, leaving little room in its nasal cavity for the roots of long canine teeth.

Even the design of the cat's skull helps in making it a successful predator. The cat's skull is wide and high, giving plenty of room to attach powerful neck muscles. During the moment of a kill, when a cat's teeth hit its prey, the impact is lessened through the cat's bones and muscles—working almost like a shock absorber. If its skull were not so well designed, the cat's neck might break from the jolt.

Most wild cats hunt in the shadows of the forest, and their dappled, spotted, or striped coats serve as camouflage. Even plain-colored cats, like the cougar and African lion, reveal their forest ancestry by giving birth to spotted cubs.

Some of the smaller, long-haired cats change their appearance when threatened. They fluff their well-furred tails, arch their backs, and assume a sideways stance to look bigger and more menacing.

A cat's fur camouflages and sometimes protects it from other animals, but not from humans, who prize cat fur for its beauty and scarcity. In the past, hunters were often the first observers of wildcats, providing much information, especially on a few smaller cats. However, many cats were being overhunted in response to demand for fur. To control this overhunting, international agreements that limit trade are now enforced, though with varying degrees of success. The cat's elusive nature, however, makes it difficult for anyone—trapper or scientist—to see many cats in the wild or to estimate their populations.

Apart from lions, cats are generally solitary hunters—and for good reason. Biologists have found that a tigress and her

During an attack, a cat automatically whips forward its retracted claws like the action of a switch-blade knife. When a cat walks, its claws remain sheathed, in a relaxed position, which prevents their being dulled.

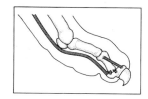

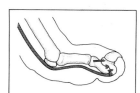

home range and *territory* are sometimes synonymous for some cats; for others, the terms mean different things, according to sex, season, and size of the area. For simplicity's sake, *home range* is generally used in this book for both terms.

Whatever it is called, a female cat's home range seems to be necessary for her to mate, to raise young in suitable den sites, and to kill enough prey to sustain herself and her young. A male's range—be it a bobcat in Colorado or a tiger in India—usually overlaps the home ranges secured by two or three females. Neighbors encounter each other along boundaries and come to know one another by sight, smell, and even voice. Even without direct contact, a threatening roar from an angry resident lion can send an intruder scurrying.

For a long time, cats were regarded as antisocial. However, some recent research has revealed that these enigmatic animals have a more complex social organization than anyone believed.

By following radio-collared ocelots, Smithsonian researcher Louise Emmons discovered that in her study area in Peru these cats had a network of social ties. On average an ocelot met another ocelot—a son, daughter, mate, or neighbor—at least once a day. Although these "solitary" cats did not tolerate a stranger in their territories, they seemed to have an established set of relationships with their resident neighbors and relatives.

When it comes to courtship in most cat species, males and females seem to seek each other out for only a few days at most. A territory-holding male's range encompasses those of several females with whom he will breed, and females may mate with several males over a period of days.

Each cat carries its own distinctive scent. Most of the scent comes from glands along the cat's tail, forehead, cheeks, and chin. Cats often spray urine mixed with glandular

three to five cubs need to eat 70 deer-sized animals in a single year. For a tiger or any other cat living in forests, hunting alone is probably the best strategy because it would be difficult for several cats to coordinate a hunt in dense cover. Lions, on the other hand, live mostly on grassy plains, where they can easily see large herds of prey such as zebras and gnus. These conditions make it more practical for lions to work as a group.

Another aid to hunting is the habit of establishing a home range—the area an animal marks for hunting, mating, sleeping, and so forth. When scientists study cats, the terms

To mark home ranges, wild cats like the cheetah (left) spray urine, make scrapes, and rub their bodies against trees and rocks as the lion and domestic cat are doing (right). The scents tell other cats the area is occupied, help males find females, and organize cat society.

secretions and scrape the ground to mark their home ranges. When a pet cat rubs its body along the sofa, it is marking its territory, just as wild cats do.

The territorial male keeps track of all the females in his home range by their scent marks and detects by changes in their scent when the females are ready to mate. Cats detect odors not only through their noses, but also through their Jacobsen's organ, a little-understood structure above the roof of the mouth. Odors are brought into contact with the Jacobsen's organ when the cat wrinkles its nose and curls its lips into a grimace known as *flehmen*.

Generally, cat courtship follows a pattern. When a new male moves in, the female at first may tussle with him. If, on the other hand, the female has often mated with a particular male before, little or no struggle may take place. Eventually she accepts the male and he mounts. In many species, the male grips the fur on the back of the female's neck in his mouth during copulation.

Apart from lionesses, most females raise their young alone, usually without any direct help from the male. Males may aid indirectly, however, by keeping a home range free of transient cats who would compete for food or harm the young.

All cats are born blind and helpless, and they instinctively snuggle in a heap while their mother is away hunting, sometimes as long as 36 hours at a time. A female raising young has to increase her hunting efforts dramatically. To satisfy her growing cubs, she needs to find and kill at least three times as much prey as when she lives alone.

Young cats grow fast, and kittens often double their body weight in a week. For the first six to eight weeks of life, kittens feed solely on milk; then their mother begins the weaning process and teaches them to hunt.

Lions and tigers often lead their cubs to kills, while smaller cats such as the ocelot may bring rodents back to the den. Many mother cats seem to give their cubs a chance to practice their hunting techniques.

Cats are sometimes described as cruel because of their habit of "playing" with live animals. However, chasing and pouncing on live prey teach a young cat how to perfect its hunting techniques.

The training period lasts several months for the smaller wild cats, and up to two years for big cats. In general, it takes longer for the cub of a big cat to reach maturity. Therefore, a young tiger, for instance, may depend on its mother for food until it is two years old, while a smaller cat, such as a bobcat, leaves home sooner.

Domestic cat owners often wonder about their cat's unsettling habit of bringing freshly killed mice or birds to the door. The cat usually gives a strange keening cry as it tries to deliver the gift, the same sound a mother cat makes when she brings food to her kittens. It seems that many housecats regard their human companions as proxy kittens and are trying to teach them what constitutes a good meal.

Though domestic cats retain many of the characteristics of their wild ancestors (see page 172), they have become more sociable. Domestic cat afficionados know that every cat exhibits a distinctive personality. Some cats come when they are called, play gently with children, and love to sleep on laps. Other cats remain aloof and distant all their lives. Whatever their personality, domestic cats have an uncanny ability to fit in with people's lives.

Though cats are kept as pets throughout the world, they are more popular in developed countries such as the United States. Maybe this holds a clue to the cat's recent surge in popularity. A domestic cat is a soft, charming companion, but in the body of an efficient, determined hunter. As we become increasingly removed from the natural world, the cat may fill a need for a touch of wildness and wilderness in our lives.

Majestic lion or urban housecat, all felines love their sleep. A lion's fitful snoozes and long naps after eating may add up to 18 to 20 hours of rest a day.

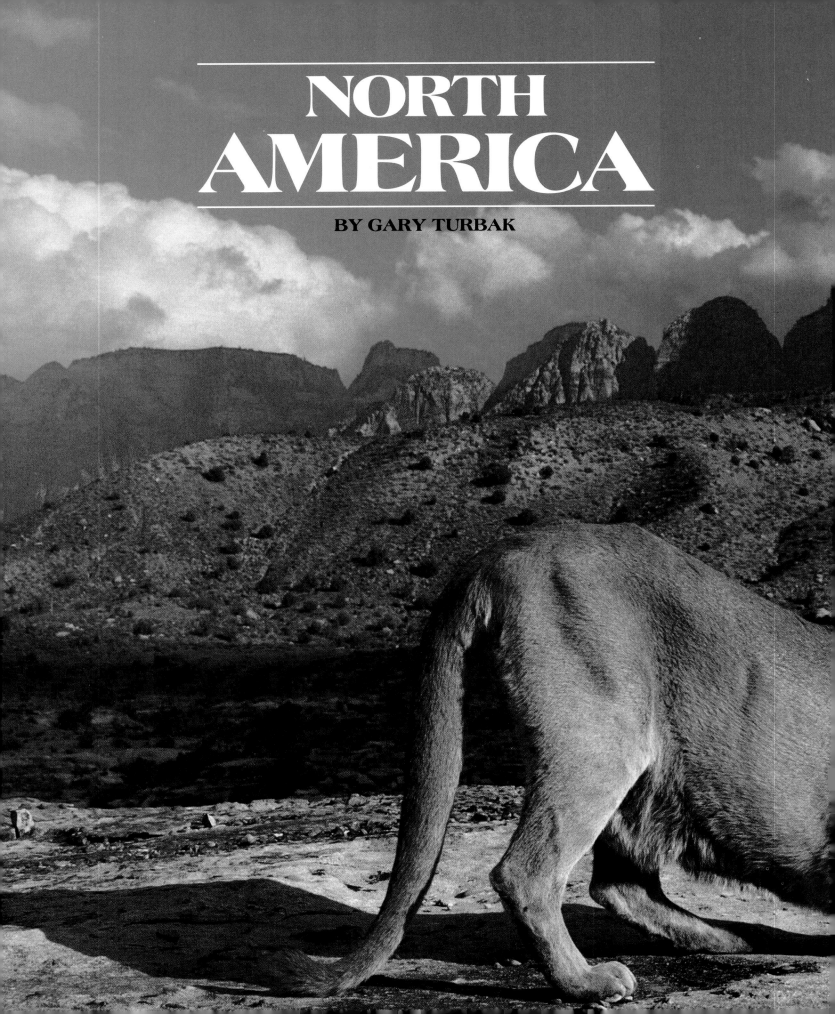

NORTH AMERICA

BY GARY TURBAK

COUGAR

Cougars range from rocky mountains to scrubby deserts, wherever prey can be found. Despite the cat's wanderings, human travelers may never spot more than paw prints among the aspen leaves (above) to confirm the cougar's presence.

Felis concolor. *Average weight: males, 160 lbs. females, 90-135 lbs.*

In the Bandelier National Monument of New Mexico, west of the Rio Grande River, past the picturesque canyons and beyond the ancient cliff dwellings, crouch two time-worn, eternal cougars. Carved from bedrock by the Cochiti Indians about the time Columbus discovered America, the life-sized stone mountain lions symbolize for us today the stormy relationship that has existed between humankind and cougars.

Great must have been the reverence that prompted ancient sculptors to create the twin effigies. Through the years, however, man has chipped away at the images just as he has savaged the living cougar, and the stone lions are gaunt reflections of their former selves. But now and then an elderly Cochiti hunter still plods to the mesa-top shrine to reaffirm the timeless bonds. And, like the flesh and blood creatures they represent, the stone lions are now protected from wanton destruction. Perhaps the cougar, stone and flesh, will last a bit longer after all.

This large North American cat goes by a number of names, including cougar, puma, mountain lion, panther, and catamount (short for cat of the mountains). Whatever the name, humans and cougars have had a topsy-turvy, roller coaster ride of a relationship. Humans have, at various times, looked upon the powerful cat with reverence, fear, hatred, awe, and admiration. One writer described the cat as "viciousness personified" with "malignant yellow eyes." But men who would have shot the cat on sight a few decades ago have reared sons and daughters who now thrill to the fleeting glimpse of a cougar. The cougar, it seems, has inspired the best and the worst in mankind.

When humans first encountered the cougar, they realized that the big cat was something special. One recurring perception of the cougar was that of a great hunter respected for its strength and agility. Soon, cougars had been incorporated into the religion or folklore of many native American tribes; the Creeks and Cherokees called the cat "Greatest of Wild Hunters," and the Chikasaws named it "Cat of God." Cougar gall, bones, and paws were believed to hold curative powers.

The cougar was the likely impetus for a pervasive native American legend. An Underwater Panther (sometimes in combination with a serpent) was said to rule the watery underworld. Humans presumably had to mediate conflict between the panther and the Thunderbird, which ruled the sky. Great Lakes tribes believed the panther's tail whipped up waves and storms. Other groups saw the Underwater Panther as a fearsome, but respected, deity.

In legend and in reality, some native Americans revered the cougar. Christian missionaries in southern California found the cougar to be a significant obstacle to establishing missions. Native Americans so respected the big cat that they refused to hunt it or to protect livestock herds from its predation. Without livestock for food and income, missions sometimes languished.

A good number of cougar stories have accumulated—some documented, some not—that paint the cat in friendly hues: frolicking like a kitten with pioneer children, or playfully following youngsters to school. In Argentina, a young woman accused of treason was said to have been tied to a tree in the wilderness to await certain death from predators. After two days, however, her punishers found her alive and well. A cougar, she said, had protected her from the jaguars and other beasts in the night.

And this story from Mexico: After a long day alone in the Coahuila desert cutting guayule (a small rubber plant), a worker became lost on his way back to camp. Then, in the light of the moon, he saw a cougar blocking his path. The man turned in another direction, but the cat moved in front of him. When the worker stepped cautiously toward

From Canada to Chile, cougars have captured human imagination. The original city of Cuzco, Peru, was laid out in the outline of a cougar, and artisans in ancient Peru laboriously hammered out golden images of the big cat (right). In North America, some Indian tribes believed in an Underwater Panther (seen on the bag below), a fearsome monster who could pull a man down to a watery grave. Even in the twentieth century, some tribes claimed such a monster cat lurked in the Mississippi River.

the animal, it retreated and waited. Again and again. Soon, the man found himself following the cougar across the desert, and in the light of dawn, he saw that the cougar had delivered him out of the wilderness.

It may have been the cougar's great hunting skill that led humans to imbue it with supernatural qualities. Or perhaps it was the cougar's stealth and secrecy. Whatever the reason, the cougar has for centuries been cloaked in mystery and mystique.

Respect for the cougar's hunting prowess and strength is well deserved. The cougar's sharp retractable claws can dig into the thickest deer or elk skin. Long canine teeth hook into a deer's tough hide, helping the cougar hang onto its prey. A single jerk of the cat's mighty forelimbs can snap an elk's neck. Reports (perhaps embellished by human imagination) claim that cougars have made vertical leaps of 15 feet and horizontal jumps of 45 feet and that a cougar cleared a nine-foot fence with a sheep in its mouth.

Naturalist Ernest Thompson Seton wrote this about cougars: "Built with the maximum power, speed, and endurance that can be jammed into his 150 pounds of lithe and splendid beasthood, his daily routine is a march of stirring athletic events that not another creature—in America, at least—can hope to equal."

Only a bit smaller than the jaguar, the cougar is the second-largest cat in the Americas. Lithe and low-slung, the cougar looks as if a "little cat" head has been set atop a "big cat" body. Males typically weigh 130 to 160 pounds and females about 90. Its coat varies from tan to dark brown, and its underparts are often white. A long, thick tail—as big around as a man's forearm—provides balance during leaps and climbs.

Historically, the cougar ranged from the Yukon to southern Chile and from the Atlantic to the Pacific. Although now its range has shrunk, it remains the most widely distributed mammal in the Americas besides man. In North America today, the cougar maintains good numbers only in the western states, Alberta, and British Columbia. Remnant or transient cats may exist in a few other states and provinces, and Florida has a small breeding population.

Except during breeding season, the cougar is a solitary animal, staking out for itself a home range that for males may cover up to 111 square miles, depending on the kind of terrain. The male's range may encompass the smaller areas of several females. Squabbles with neighbors are rare, since each cat usually honors the boundaries that other cougars have marked. Scrapes and urine are the traditional signposts. A male cougar piles pine needles, leaves, or dirt with his hind feet, then tops it off with a splash of urine or a deposit of feces. Females cover their deposits.

At any time of year, cougars may mate when the male detects hormonal cues from the female in heat. The male departs soon after and takes no responsibility for caring for the resulting kittens. Males do, however, seem to stabilize the social environment by repelling transient male cougars.

In a cave or rock den, the mother gives birth to two or three spotted kittens who show little hint of the powerful creatures they will later become. At birth, the kittens are blind, weigh a pound or less, and stretch all of 12 inches long. In two weeks, their eyes open. At six weeks, they may go to their first kill, but as observers only. At six months, their spots begin to disappear, a process that can take several months, and they become *Felis concolor*—cats of one color.

The cubs, like those of most large carnivores, have a lot to learn before they become successful predators. The young generally stay with the mother until they are about 20 to 22 months old, picking up tricks of the trade on how to stalk rabbits or deer, practicing their moves and timing. Then they must find home ranges of their own.

John W. Audubon, 1840s.

DO COUGARS "SCREAM"?

Despite all that has been learned about cougars, a bit of mystery still clings to the cat. Outdoorsmen can still get into a good argument about "the scream." Does the cat roll its head back and cut loose with a bloodcurdling wail? Or is that part of the cougar mystique?

Early settlers certainly thought the scream was for real, comparing it to the sound of a woman being attacked.

One summer day on the Missouri frontier, an entire community did indeed cringe at the screaming of an unseen giant cougar. Women and children scurried indoors, while the men rode out to do battle. Ever louder screams warned the posse that the "monster cougar" must be moving along the river bank. Then around the final bend it came—a newfangled, whistle-blowing steamboat named the *Flora Jones*.

Cougars do emit sounds ranging from yowls to birdlike whistles. Some cougar experts, however, believe that virtually all "screams" may be cases of mistaken identity.

Maurice Hornocker, after 20 years of cougar study, has never heard a cougar scream. "They certainly don't emit the 'attacked woman' sound," he says. "Those sounds probably come from foxes, coyotes, or owls." Only the cougar knows for sure, and perhaps it's good to let the cat keep a few secrets.

Despite the mother cougar's care, not all cubs will make it to adulthood, depending on how much prey the mother can get, and whether she survives hunters and disease.

Rather than driving her nearly-mature offspring away, the mother seems to put them in a situation where they are forced to make it on their own. Zoologist John Seidensticker recounts one instance when the mother cougar took her young to a kill and then left them there, disappearing far back into her own area where she soon mated with another cougar. The young did not rejoin the mother, and eventually set out in search of their own home ranges.

Typically, a cougar travels alone seeking sight or sound of its favorite prey—deer. For a cougar to patrol all of its huge home range might take up to two days, so rather than fooling around with unproductive areas, a cougar concentrates on areas where it has frequently found prey before.

Blend curiosity and caution, and you have the ingredients of a good predator-to-be. Probing and playing with living things, such as a turtle (top), give a cougar cub valuable experience in the art of choosing prey. Trying to pin down a rodent (above) echoes the domestic cat's play with a rolling ball of twine.

The mother cougar spends almost two years raising her cubs to independence. Young adults (right) eventually must set out to find their own home range.

For this deer, death from the cougar's powerful bite to the neck comes mercifully quickly. In North America, deer and rabbits provide most of a cougar's sustenance. A cougar may kill a deer every two weeks, but this varies with weather and the cat's hunting skill. A mother with cubs needs even more, perhaps a deer every three days, or seven jackrabbits a day.

Rarely do cougars lurk in the treetops. Rather, a cougar moves efficiently through its territory until a slight sound or movement betrays the presence of prey. Then in slow motion, the cougar creeps as close as it can. When it gets so close that the next step might alert the prey, the cat charges. In two or three fluid, lightning-quick bounds it catches its prey, using an arsenal of teeth, claws, and strength to dispatch the victim. Frequently, the stalk and kill are so efficient that a deer dies in the spot where it bedded down.

Cougars have an eclectic diet, generally eating what they encounter, when they encounter it. When deer bunch together in the winter, cougars find and eat more deer. In summer, when deer scatter more widely, the cougar adds rabbits, birds, porcupines, squirrels, racoons, rats, and even grasshoppers to the menu. Sheep, cattle, and other livestock also fall victim now and then to a hungry cougar, but not as often as some ranchers may think. In parts of the West, cougars and livestock live in harmony on the same public land. Most cougar predation on livestock occurs in the southwestern United States, and studies are underway to determine if that is due to scarcity of prey or to some other reason.

The cougar's hunting prowess is best put in perspective by comparing body weights of predator and prey. When deer are not available, a cougar can kill an elk or moose six or seven times as large as itself.

Predation is an iffy business, though, and every successful stalk may be preceded by several failures. A cougar may hit 40 mph in a sprint, but it has little stamina and must catch its prey in a few bounds or give up.

Once a cat has committed itself to an attack, the battle has just begun. Elk have trampled cougars to death and have snapped their necks by flinging them against trees. Researchers once discovered a cougar skull with a piece of tree limb still penetrating its brain cavity. They guessed that the cat suffered the lethal blow during an attack on a deer or elk. They also have found the decaying carcasses of a cougar and a mule deer side by side—indicating that the two animals probably fought to their mutual deaths. Cougars who make it to adulthood may live eleven years or more if they escape such encounters with other animals—and with humans. For aside from old age, legal hunting is the number one cause of cougar deaths.

Through the years, the cougar has had its troubles with humankind. The respect that many native Americans afforded the cat was not generally shared by Europeans who later emigrated to North America. Perhaps cougar attacks on livestock (and even rarer ones on humans) led to a sort of cultural hysteria. Perhaps the newcomers simply feared a powerful animal they seldom saw and did not understand.

Whatever the causes, cougar loathing sank solid roots in the new colonies. As early as 1694, Connecticut was paying a 20-shilling bounty for a dead cougar. Other colonies later followed suit, and cougar hatred grew to a fever pitch.

One incident illustrates the extent to which cougar hysteria gripped the pioneers. Upon going to frontier Oklahoma and being regaled with cougar stories, a young cowboy slept only fitfully for fear of being attacked by a cougar. One night an eerie cry roused him. Certain that a cougar was about to attack the camp, he readied his pistol. Suddenly, in the darkness just beyond the campfire's glow, a pair of evil-looking eyes appeared, and the terrified greenhorn fired. When the dust settled, it was the cook's old hound, not a marauding cougar, that lay dead.

As European immigrants moved west across North America, they killed cougars at every opportunity. Declining deer numbers and the cutting down of forests also augured ill for the cougar. Faced with loss of cover and prey, populations in the East plummeted.

Like lights in a corridor going out one by

Though they may have a penchant for traveling the night trails, cougars are round-the-clock predators, stalking to within a few yards of unsuspecting prey.

the protection of closed hunting seasons and restricted bag limits. One 1983 study shows cougars present in 23 states, and protected there to at least some degree. Half of the 23 states allow no hunting or trapping at all.

Much of what we know about the cougar in today's new light has come to us courtesy of Maurice Hornocker, dean of cougar researchers. In the early 1960s, no one—not even scientists and wildlife managers—knew very much about the big cat. So Hornocker, then a young biologist, set out on what would later become one of the world's classic wildlife studies. He took with him an expert woodsman, Wilbur Wiles, and his dogs.

Hornocker and Wiles plunged into the vast River of No Return Wilderness in Idaho. Over the next ten winters, they (and the graduate students who later joined them) logged thousands of snowshoe miles in some of the most rugged terrain in North America. Because radio collars had not yet been perfected in a wilderness setting, the best way for Hornocker to learn about a cougar was to tree it with hounds, drug it, mark it, release it, then hope to catch it again later. By the study's end, he had captured 64 different cougars more than 300 times.

Two surprising discoveries came from Hornocker's work. First, he learned that cougars tend to restrict their own numbers with a complex system of territoriality that prevents any area from being overrun with cats. More important, cougars in his study area did not closely control deer and elk populations. "Most often, a cougar will kill a deer or elk that is less fit, either behaviorally or physically," says Hornocker. "If prey populations are healthy, then the cougar isn't going to have much effect."

Hornocker's discoveries played an important role in helping the cat rebound from the age of persecution. Today, many people lucky enough to glimpse a cougar in the wild are thrilled, not terrified.

In the East, forests and deer have both

one, the cougar quietly disappeared from most eastern and midwestern states. With a few exceptions, the beginning of the twentieth century saw the cougar remaining only in the rugged lands of the West, perhaps saved only by the forbidding wilderness in which it lived.

Then in mid-century, the wind of public opinion began to shift. Reborn in the new notion that predators are not inherently evil, cougar esteem grew with a fresh vigor. In 1958, British Columbia dropped its bounty. In 1965, Colorado reclassified the cougar from varmint to game animal. By 1970, all bounties had disappeared.

To be sure, the woods are not filled with smiling, reformed cougar hunters. Yet the tide has turned, and today the cougar enjoys

The powerful cougar will take on all comers—well, almost all. It is terrified of barking dogs, and even a yapping poodle could perhaps send a cougar scrambling for a tree.

returned, creating huge tracts of excellent cougar habitat. Yet the question of the cat's eastern presence is hotly debated. A few cougar holdouts may have survived there all these years, but proof is hard to come by.

Wildlife authorities put up 1,000 "wanted posters" (asking for reports of cougar sightings) in forests, country stores, and schools. They baited scent stations with catnip and surrounded them with sand to record tracks. They collected likely looking scats in plastic bags and shipped them off to laboratories for possible identification. They even trucked into the mountains a female cougar in heat to see if she might attract a wild male.

Researchers also checked plenty of tracks and remains, most of which turned out to be those of dogs, coyotes, or housecats. Once, the corpse of a huge feline was discovered, but it proved to be an African lion that had escaped from a nearby zoo.

In Great Smoky Mountains National Park, employees watched a cougar stalking deer. People reported seeing a female with kittens along the Blue Ridge Parkway in North Carolina. A Georgia hunter stared in disbelief as a cougar stalked the same turkeys he was hunting. But such accounts—even from expert observers—do not a cougar make. Even a photo or a track would not prove the existence of a resident population of cats. So far, then, nothing proves the cat's presence in the East, and even the most persistent searchers are beginning to despair.

In Florida, meanwhile, hope for a healthy cougar population runs stronger. The state's southern swamps and forests harbor a small population of panthers, which is what the cat is called there. Though almost identical to the cougar of the West, the Florida panther has distinct characteristics, such as longer limbs and a different cranial structure, that identify it as a separate subspecies. With fewer than 100 in existence, it is one of the rarest mammals in North America.

To prevent its extinction, wildlife officials have attached radio collars to panthers so that data on home ranges and other characteristics can be gathered. To curtail road kills, some highways now have concrete underpasses for the cats. "I really believe most people in Florida would like to see the panther saved," says Chris Belden, the Florida biologist in charge of the project. "But there are those who will shoot [illegally] the first one they see."

Contrary to popular opinion of a few decades ago, the cougar is virtually no threat to campers, hikers, and other frequenters of cougar habitat. Since 1900 in North America, only seven human deaths from cougar attacks have been documented.

Other reports of cougar killings have proved false. In 1934, hunters in British Columbia killed a cougar and found in its stomach scraps of blue cloth and two buttons emblazoned with an anchor. They quickly concluded the cougar had eaten a sailor. Newspapers proclaimed killer cougars were about, and armed guards stood watch.

Then one day, a man in sailor garb came to the police and identified the buttons. His jacket had become soaked with whale oil, he said, and he had tossed it in the garbage. The "man-eating" cougar had been guilty of nothing more than plundering a garbage can.

Even Theodore Roosevelt, who had no love for the cougar, knew that humans had little to fear. "I should have no more hesitation in sleeping out in a wood where there were cougars than I should have if the cougars were tomcats," he wrote.

There seems little reason, then, that humans and cougars cannot peacefully coexist. Perhaps deep in unrecorded history a kinship existed between man and cougar. Perhaps that is why a cougar, be it flesh or legend, occasionally deigns to guard a maiden in the wilderness or to guide a thirsty soul out of the desert. Perhaps the cat remembers what we cannot. Perhaps.

Fewer than 100 Florida panthers (right) exist, making the steely-eyed cat one of the most endangered mammals in the United States.

BOBCAT

The deer hunter's rest beneath the pine tree turned into a nap. Then, some presence caused him to awaken, and while the sleep was draining from his mind, he saw a cat watching him from across the clearing. The animal showed no fear, no aggression. It only sat there on its haunches, staring with its haunting yellow eyes. As the hunter became fully alert, the cat vanished like a wisp of smoke.

This kind of fleeting communion is about as close as most people can ever hope to come to the bobcat. Humans making regular forays into bobcat country should consider themselves lucky if they have such an ephemeral encounter more than once or twice in a lifetime. It's a bit surprising, therefore, to learn that the elusive bobcat has lately spawned a controversy.

Native only to North America, the bobcat's taste for venison, lamb, and chicken did nothing to endear it to humans, and most of the early colonies established bounties to reward people who killed bobcats. Compared to the cougar, however, the bobcat has not been so fiercely hated or persecuted.

Scientists paid it little heed until a number of studies in the 1950s. Then during the 1970s, several things happened to push the bobcat to prominence. First, a burgeoning interest in ecology and the environment increased public appreciation for all wildlife, even predators. In 1975, an international agreement (the Convention on International Trade in Endangered Species of Wild Fauna and Flora—CITES) prohibited the export of the skins of endangered species such as leopard, ocelot, and cheetah. This caused European furriers to look toward the bobcat and other small cats as replacements.

While trappers and hunters moved to cash in on the new bonanza in bobcat fur, conservationists and wildlife managers plowed through a series of court cases to determine who should manage the bobcats and how it should be done. These questions needed to be answered because CITES said the bobcat might become endangered if export of its fur was not regulated.

As a result of this activity, statewide bounties on bobcats have been dropped. Regulated hunting and trapping seasons are now the norm, and in some places the cat is completely protected. States that once ignored the bobcat or paid citizens to kill it now spend money on bobcat management.

Bobcats now range from southern Canada through most of the United States and into Mexico. The only U.S. region without bobcats is a belt that runs from central South Dakota through the Great Lakes states to the Atlantic. Urban sprawl and intensive agriculture have driven bobcats out of some places where they once lived.

Just who is this wraithlike cat that has caused such a stir? The bobcat is a secretive predator that minds its own business and only rarely has any effect on humans. Weighing about 20 pounds, the bobcat is usually reddish- or yellowish-brown with splotches of black mottling its thick fur. A stubby, 6-inch tail gives the animal its name.

Other features are long legs, a ruff of facial fur, and a tuft of hair rising from the tip of each ear. While the long ear tufts look like miniature antennas, they also may serve as visual cues that help bobcats communicate with each other, according to one researcher.

The female bobcat is territorial, staking out for herself a home range that varies in individual cats from less than 2 to more than 40 square miles. With urine, scent from anal glands, and feces, bobcats put up olfactory "no trespassing" signs along the boundaries of their home ranges. Females' home ranges almost never overlap. Males, on the other hand, frequently share parts of a large home range with both sexes. The amount of food available seems to be the number one factor in determining the extent of the overlap.

During hard times, bobcats may compromise, as researcher Ted Bailey discovered. In

Kittens face an uncertain future, depending on the bobcat mother's luck in hunting. Foxes and owls may snatch young from the den, too. Yet a young adult (far right) is more vulnerable than a kitten, for it must find its own range.

Idaho one winter, freezing temperatures and a scarcity of rabbits forced two males and two females to abandon their hermit-like lifestyle. They still hunted on their own, but they shared the same rockpile den until the weather broke a few days later.

During the winter breeding season, the two sexes seek each other briefly, then go their separate ways. The female is left to raise the kittens (usually about three) by herself. Some evidence suggests that when there are more female bobcats than home ranges, those females without suitable home ranges do not breed. Harsh conditions can also force harsh—at least to humans—responses. During lean times, bobcat mothers have been known to abandon their young, sensing it was time to cut their losses and get food only for themselves.

By late winter, young bobcats, now about eleven months old, have set out in search of a home range they can call their own.

Bobcats can thrive from swampland to wooded mountainside, eating a variety of prey. The bobcat's adaptability to habitat and prey has made it the most numerous wild cat in the Americas. Keen eyes and ears, ambushes, and short bursts of speed make the bobcat a consummate small-game predator. No matter what its habitat, the bobcat's diet is first and foremost rabbits. Day in, day out, about 80 percent of its diet is rabbits. Yet it also eats mice, deer fawns, fish, and even carrion. When it's hungry, the bobcat doesn't even hesitate to take on adult deer.

Killing a healthy adult deer that can weigh 150 pounds is an ambitious undertaking for a bobcat that probably doesn't weigh 25 pounds wringing wet. Because the bobcat is so small, it stands the best chance of killing a deer if it can attack the prey in its bed. Even then, it's likely that the deer is able to get to its feet, which accounts for tales told over the years by woodsmen who claim to have seen a deer racing through the forest with a biting, clawing bobcat perched atop its back. No one knows how many healthy, adult deer bobcats kill, but the cat probably does not play a significant role in deer population dynamics.

The modern image of the bobcat is not so much that of marauding predator, but rather that of a ghost. The animal's interaction with humans usually consists of a fleeting encounter in the cat's terrain on the cat's terms. "Suddenly I was staring into the face of a bobcat from a distance of about 15 feet," recalls one sportsman. "There was something eerie in the event. The cat had quietly materialized out of the air itself. No rustling of leaves or whisking of palmetto or gallberry bush. Just suddenly that staring, yellow-eyed presence. I fumbled with the camera, and the cat dissolved into nothing."

Even biologists who spend months tracking bobcats in the field rarely see one of them. But the cats know they are there, and it is not unusual for researchers to find bobcat tracks superimposed on their footprints. "At times I wonder who is following whom,"

A bobcat's diet is adaptive perfection. If cottontail rabbits are plentiful, the bobcat eats those. But if fish, rats, or birds are easier to get, the cat accordingly changes the menu.

says Canadian biologist Alison Evans, who spent several weeks studying bobcats.

If given an escape route, the bobcat will run instead of wrangle. Yet when flight turns to fight, the ghost can get its dander up.

During one study, a bobcat escaped by carrying off a leg-hold trap with the offset jaws still clamped on one foot. Biologist Michael O'Brien and his hound tracked the cat, and the dog rushed in—and then out. Repeatedly, the exceptionally large bobcat (32 pounds) rebuffed with ease the charges of the 75-pound hound. "It could easily have killed my dog, even with the trap still on its foot," recalls the incredulous O'Brien. The cantankerous frontiersman who boasted that he could lick his weight in wildcats would have come out shredded if he had ever tried.

Like most cats, the bobcat reveals a curious side, too. Tracks in the snow show that the cats frequently detour off the trail to investigate some sight or sound, or maybe just to have the pleasure of walking the length of a fallen log. They've also been seen rolling a stone playfully across bare ground the way a housecat might play with a ball, swatting at insects on a mud puddle, and leaping just for the pleasure of leaping.

Anything from a shiny piece of metal to a whiff of a man's after-shave lotion might attract the curious cats. This means that they are not particularly difficult to trap, and that has led to the bobcat controversy.

Anti-hunting and anti-trapping groups have pushed for a halt to bobcat killing. Other groups, including many wildlife agencies, argue that no new decisions on killing should be made until it is better known how many cats exist. Wildlife agencies argue that bobcats are impossible to count and that comparing the number killed from year to year provides the best indication of relative abundance or scarcity. This information can be supplemented by research, including monitoring tracks, tagging pelts, and studying scent station visitations.

As the debate over population figures goes on, 37 states allow killing of the cats, and the number of pelts recorded remains high. In 1987, a short bobcat coat could be bought in the United States for $5,000 to $6,000. Bobcat skins are the most heavily traded in the world—about 84,000 were sold in 1984.

"The bobcat has proven to be resilient and adaptable, but that doesn't mean its future is guaranteed," says S. Douglas Miller, an ecologist and vice president of the National Wildlife Federation. "Bobcats can survive only if resource management authorities remain diligent in monitoring bobcat populations, habitat, and harvest."

Whether the adaptable bobcat, survivor of decades of bounties, can hold its own remains to be seen. While habitat loss and harvest pressure take their toll, responsible planning and management should ensure that many more generations of bobcats will be around to create eerie moments for people lucky enough to come face to face with this phantom of the forest.

LYNX

Always at home in the deep northern woods, the lynx is essentially a solitary hunter.

Lynx canadensis. *Average weight: 22-25 lbs.*

In a bed beneath a hanging bough of fir, the lynx stirs. The early evening sky of southern Ontario is turning darker, and it is time for the cat to be about its business. Like a housecat, the lynx stretches, then rakes its claws across a log to sharpen them. Now free of sleep, it slips into the snowy silence of the woodland north.

For centuries, the lynx has puzzled mankind—appearing where it should not be, showing little fear of humans, agile yet slow to flee, plentiful one decade and scarce the next. To human beings the lynx seems a bit strange: solitary, curious, something that might at any time be watching from the shadows. Even the lynx's name evokes a touch of beauty and mystery. "Lynx" is from a Greek word meaning "to shine," possibly chosen because of the reflective quality of the cat's eyes.

Today, of course, science has given the lynx a flesh and blood identity, shedding light on its biology but doing nothing to lessen its intrigue.

The lynx is a denizen of the northern woods, preferring dense forest and thicket to open parkland and meadow. It exists in the Soviet Union, Scandinavia, Poland, China, and in other Asian and European countries (see page 122). In North America, the lynx is essentially Canadian, living everywhere except Prince Edward Island and thriving in most provinces except Nova Scotia and New Brunswick. In the United States, its range includes Alaska, parts of the northern tier of states and a few mountain areas in Colorado, Wyoming, Washington, and Utah.

While the lynx and bobcat are nearly twin phantoms (see box, page 56), the lynx has unusually broad feet. The hindquarters are so high that one observer called the lynx "an animal that appeared to be walking downhill when walking on the level."

The lynx's social structure and land tenure system do not seem to follow a set pattern. Both sexes do maintain home ranges that

vary from 6 to 19 square miles, but the ranges often overlap. Hostility seems limited to members of the same sex. Female lynx produce one litter (usually two to four kittens) a year and get no help from the male during the months of raising the offspring.

Through woods flecked with filtered moonlight the lynx travels—sometimes at a walk, sometimes on the trot. The powdery snow makes no sound beneath his feet. Driven by a growling belly now three days empty, he seeks the snowshoe hare.

At some point in its evolution, the lynx hitched its star to the snowshoe hare, and the bond has held. Though it will deign to eat other prey, ranging from small birds to caribou, the lynx needs the hare to survive. "It lives on rabbits, follows the rabbits, thinks rabbits, increases with them, and on their failure dies of starvation in the unrabbited woods," wrote naturalist Ernest Thompson Seton in 1925.

Canadian records going back more than 200 years show clearly how close the

relationship is. Periodically, the hare population plummets, often because of disease or weather. When it does, times get tough for the lynx, which must capture what it can of other prey. The lynx soon fails to reproduce, and within a couple of years becomes scarce. Eventually, the hare rebounds and becomes more numerous. The lynx, like a shadow, follows suit. When hares are abundant, lynx become prolific, producing three to six young a year with little mortality among the kits. However, when food shortage, disease, or some genetic factor precipitates another dramatic fall in the hare population, the whole saga begins again. From peak to peak, the cycle lasts about 10 years.

Only recently have scientists discovered how the hare shortage forces the lynx into a population decline. "There seems to be some minimum density of hares below which a female lynx is not capable of successfully rearing kittens," says researcher Lloyd Keith. The adults continue to mate, but the female may fail to conceive. If kittens are born, they may starve while the female consumes all the prey she catches.

Why the numbers of snowshoe hares fluctuate may be another story. One hypothesis, under study at the Institute for Arctic Biology in Alaska, points to the hare's diet. The hare's favorite food is the feltleaf willow, but only mature willows are

nutritious. When mature willows are over-browsed, the willow responds by producing unpalatable young shoots. Consequently, the hare population drops. As the snowshoe goes, so goes the lynx.

When hare populations are low, adult lynx don't wait around to starve. They strike out in all directions in search of a greater population of hares. An average night's travel might be about eight miles when prey is plentiful and the weather is good, or 20 miles when conditions are poor.

Because hare shortages are local, not universal, the cats are sometimes successful without traveling far. If not, they keep going—sometimes out of the woods, and even into cities. In the early 1960s and again a decade later, lynx showed up in places like Edmonton, Alberta, and Winnipeg, Manitoba. The distance record appears to belong to a Yukon lynx that traveled 500 miles in seven months after hare numbers dropped severely on its home range.

Near the junction of several hare trails, the lynx selects a hiding spot and waits in ambush. Periodically, the cat shifts to point in another direction, and eventually creates a circular hunting bed. Finally, a hare bounds over the snow. The cat's body tenses, then releases like a coiled spring. In a few seconds it is over, and the lynx eats.

Hare hunting is no easy chore. Four of every five hares the lynx pursues may escape, and the cat needs one about every other day to survive. To find food, the lynx often has to travel miles between kills. A large prey such as a deer would replace many hares, but it would take seven red squirrels to supply the food value of just one hare.

Besides waiting in ambush for prey (and even, on rare occasions, dropping out of a tree onto a deer's back), the lynx employs its keen sight and hearing to locate a meal. Like most cats, a lynx needs to capture its quarry in a few bounds or give up the chase. Stamina plays no part in the lynx's attack, although a hungry cat will pursue its prey longer than a cat that is well fed.

The lynx, like most cats, is a loner. However, females and their nearly grown offspring do sometimes hunt together. Tracks in the snow show that when they approach a promising chunk of hare habitat, the cats fan out. If a hare escapes from one lynx, it may well run into the jaws of another.

Because of its four-inch broad paws (right), the lynx can easily match the snowshoe hare's ability to travel over deep snow. A lynx may kill a hare every other day. As the supply of hares rises or falls, however, so goes the lynx population.

TWIN PHANTOMS

In Canada, the lynx and the bobcat are almost look-alikes, sporting the same gray and brown mottled fur, facial ruff, stubby tail, and ear tufts. "If I were to see a wild cat just briefly in the field, I could not be sure if it were a lynx or a bobcat," says Gerry Parker, a Canadian biologist who has studied both animals.

If the cats could be seen side by side, however, the lynx's broader, snowshoelike paws; longer legs; and longer ear tufts would distinguish it from the bobcat. The long, glossy black ear tufts may increase the lynx's hearing ability or, when moved in a certain way, they may act as a signal to other lynxes.

In body shape, the lynx appears more streamlined than the bobcat, although both cats weigh about 15 to 25 pounds. Their tails also differ, the lynx's having a black tip, while the markings on the bobcat's can vary.

It may be easier to tell the difference with a map than with the human eye. Biologists believe that the lynx and bobcat have divided the continent between them along a line roughly following the Canada-United States border. Because of its wide paws and ability to travel in deep snow, the lynx is more at home in the northern woods, while the bobcat is more numerous in warmer climates.

The lynx dominates the Canadian northland because it has the footgear to travel in deep snow. When a hard crust forms on the snow, the lynx's chase after a hare becomes even easier.

The lynx's huge paws are fully four inches in diameter, and act as snowshoes. Hair fills the spaces between the toes, so the cat's paw does an excellent job of keeping the animal from floundering in deep snow. In field tests, biologist Gerry Parker found that the huge paws of the lynx support about twice as much weight in snow as do the bobcat's.

The lynx has long had the reputation of being docile when it becomes the prey. Naturalist Adolph Murie, who studied wildlife in Alaska over three decades, thought part of the lynx's tameness might be due to its reliance on escaping discovery. After observing one lynx, Murie noted, "I looked up the slope for him, and wondered where he could have gone, for no cover was nearby. Then, from among the rocks 20 paces off, he bounded away. He had blended with the boulders in the evening shade."

The lynx also is fairly easy to trap, and during the first half of this century, overtrapping eliminated the cat from parts of the U.S. and thinned its ranks in southern Canada. In the 1960s and early 1970s, lynx numbers rebounded and appeared to stabilize.

However, recent demand for spotted fur (precipitated by the ban on the use of cat pelts from other parts of the world) has again caused some worry about the long-term future of the lynx. Some people fear that if high demand for lynx fur coincides with a cyclic low in cat numbers, the result could be the elimination of the lynx from some areas. For now, though, the cat seems secure.

As dawn edges into the forest, the lynx beds down atop a knoll. Tracks in the snow tell it that hares not long ago passed this way. Perhaps the next meal will come easy. If not, the lynx will again rise to go into the wilderness and hunt.

LATIN AMERICA

BY FIONA SUNQUIST

JAGUAR

In a burst of black and gold, a jaguar emerges from the darkness of a Central American forest (left). Largest of the Latin American cats, the jaguar masters all dimensions—it climbs, it swims, and it roams dense forests with ease.

Panthera onca. *Weight: males, 120-200 lbs. females, 80-100 lbs.*

The sun created the jaguar to be his representative on earth. He gave him the yellow coat of his power and he gave him the voice of thunder which is the voice of God.

— Tucaño Amazon Indian myth

Commanding fear and respect throughout Latin America, the jaguar looms larger than life. Ever since the Olmecs created one of the earliest known Central American civilizations, the jaguar has appeared as a symbol throughout Latin American art, religion, and culture. From Mexico to the Andes, jaguar images appeared in nearly every cultural facet of early indigenous peoples.

Thousands of years ago, the Olmecs built elaborate monuments to this jungle deity, carving massive 20-ton stone heads of jaguars. The Aztec and Mayan civilizations incorporated Olmec were-jaguars—half man, half jaguar—into their culture and religion. The jaguar was also embodied in mosaics, textiles, ornaments, and figurines. The animal itself was sought for its hide and whatever magical properties its hair, teeth, bones, and blood might imbue. Even today, some Indian tribes practice man-jaguar rituals using drugs and incantations.

All the big cats have inspired their share of myths and legends, but few have played such a pivotal role in the religion and culture of a continent as the jaguar. Why did these ancient Latin American people choose the jaguar totem as the central theme of their culture? What is it about the jaguar that continues to fascinate people today?

The jaguar is the largest cat in the western hemisphere, but it was more than size which impressed the Indians. For the Indians the jaguar embodied immeasurable power. They named it *yaguara,* which loosely translated means "a beast that kills its prey with one bound." The jaguar might be good or it might be evil, but above all, it was powerful. Scientist Charles Darwin, visiting South America on the 1833 voyage of the *Beagle,*

confessed that "the fear of the [jaguar] quite destroyed all pleasure in scrambling through the woods. I had not proceeded a hundred yards before finding indubitable signs. . . . I was obliged to come back."

The jaguar is the ultimate predator, the dominant power in the forest, an animal that uses its strength and cunning to overcome other animals. The jaguar masters all dimensions—it climbs, it swims, and it roams the densest forests. For the largest predator in the Americas, almost no prey is too ambitious a target. Although some adult tapirs weigh 650 pounds and thus may escape the jaguar's attack, nearly everything else is vulnerable to its awesome strength.

The jaguar's robust power has given it the reputation of being immense. In reality, however, jaguars are smaller than legend or looks would have people believe. Though male jaguars weighing nearly 300 pounds have been documented, the average jaguar weighs less. In Mexico, Belize, and Peru, adult males commonly weigh around 120 pounds and females average 80 pounds, or roughly the weight of a German shepherd dog. The biggest jaguars have been found in Brazil's Pantanal, a vast plain. There, males regularly top the scales at more than 200 pounds, while females can weigh as much as 170 pounds.

Large or small, the jaguar gives the impression of unassailable power. Even a 70 pound jaguar looks as if it could overpower an ox. The jaguar does not have the lithe build and sinuous grace so characteristic of its Asian cousin, the leopard. The jaguar is a strong, stocky cat, deep chested with a large, rounded head and short sturdy limbs. Even the jaguar's canine teeth seem stronger than those of the other great cats, and its killing technique reflects the extraordinary strength of its muscles and teeth.

Lions, tigers, and leopards usually kill their prey with a throat or neck bite. Jaguars, on the other hand, often bite *through* the

The jaguar (below), at home in many habitats, can live in mountainous altitudes up to 8,000 feet, in grassland and scrub areas, and in lowland rainforests.

A young jaguar's coat (right) begins to show the coloration and rosette markings of an adult. Weighing about two pounds at birth, cubs grow under their mother's tutelage for about two years, then strike out on their own.

temporal bones of the skull, between the ears of prey such as capybara or peccary. Even the very thick skulls of such animals are no obstacle to a hungry jaguar, whose teeth punch through with little trouble.

One of the naturalists who accompanied Theodore Roosevelt on his Brazilian expedition in the early 1900s examined a six-foot caiman killed by a jaguar. He surmised the jaguar had crunched the crocodile's neck vertebrae with its powerful jaws, then torn open the paralyzed reptile's chest.

Jaguars can kill smaller animals such as dogs just by slapping them with a paw. Animals killed in this way usually have no signs of external injury; they usually die of a crushed skull.

After visiting South America in the early 1800s, French naturalist Baron Georges Cuvier reported that "the natives assert that [jaguars] sleep and often lay wait for their prey on trees; and from this circumstance, they derive the name of *Dahan*, which signifies the fork formed by the branch of a tree." Today, though, we know most of the jaguar's hunting is probably done on the ground. Like most of the big cats, jaguars usually hunt by walking along a well-used trail or beside a stream crossing until they encounter prey, then stalking or rushing it. Occasionally, jaguars do wait in ambush, leaping on unsuspecting prey as they pass. Now and then, jaguars may take to the trees to grab a monkey.

Despite all its strength and power, the jaguar subsists mainly on a diet of smaller prey. The jaguar does not discriminate, however, and devours whatever is available: lizards, snakes, peccaries, capybara, turtles, fish, small rodents, deer, birds, caimans, or whatever else may fall in its path. In the lowlands of Venezuela and Brazil, jaguars

Black jaguars (right) are not another species but a melanistic variation. Upon looking closely, the black color is not solid black after all, but simply a dark background color and black spots that appear to meld together.

feed mainly on capybara, a semi-aquatic rodent that can weigh about 100 pounds. This bristly-coated animal swims and dives well and usually swarms in herds along Latin American rivers, streams, and lakes. One writer said, "The capybara is the jaguar's daily bread." J. R. Rengger, who watched a jaguar hunt capybara, reported in the early 1800s that, "Serpent-like the jaguar winds its way over the ground, often making a considerable detour to approach from another direction where there is less risk of being detected. The capybara may get the stalker's wind when it is still far away and will rush into the water, uttering cries of alarm. Jaguars have been seen to jump into the river after a capybara and catch it before it could dive to safety."

Though turtles may seem rather unlikely prey for a big cat, they form an important part of the jaguar's diet. Female river turtles coming ashore to lay their eggs are particularly vulnerable. Although jaguars usually break the carapace while feeding on these armored reptiles, they sometimes display considerable finesse, scooping out the meat without even cracking the shell. Empty, overturned turtle shells with traces of jaguar hair often litter beaches where turtles nest.

The jaguar's fishing methods have been the subject of considerable debate. According to Indian folk tales, "the jaguar goes a little way out into the water, and there discharges some saliva, which attracts the fish, which the jaguar flips out onto the bank with his paw." Other accounts maintain that jaguars lure fish by tapping on the water with their tails. Two naturalists in the mid-1800s were told by Indians that when a jaguar raps the surface of the water with his tail, he imitates the sound of falling fruit to lure fruit-eating fish. Quite a few fruit-eating fish do exist in the Amazon, and they are attracted to the sound of fruit falling into the water, so this story holds some credence.

Whether jaguars intentionally use their tail and saliva as lures is debatable. Most cats twitch their tails as they watch their prey, and a fishing jaguar is probably no exception. A twitching tail, or droplets of saliva, might accidentally attract fruit-eating fish; however, it is unlikely that the jaguar performs either of these actions for the express purpose of attracting fish.

Jaguars probably do take advantage of fish wherever they can find them. In the wetlands of Venezuela and Brazil, for instance, large fish often breed in shallow pools. As the dry season progresses, the pools dry out, leaving the fish stranded and vulnerable to storks and other predators.

Most of the jaguar's small prey are scattered through the forest, singly or in small groups. Herds of large game do not roam the jaguar's usual haunts.

In North America 12,000 years ago, the jaguar roamed from Oregon to Pennsylvania. Remains have been found from Alaska to Mexico, and 76 jaguar skeletons were recovered from the La Brea tar pits in California. Though it presumably had disappeared from the mid-Atlantic region before Columbus' time, the jaguar continued to survive in the West and in some of the southeastern states until quite recently.

On a hunting trip in 1855, Grizzly Adams encountered a jaguar in the Tehachapi Mountains in southern California. Adams wrote that, "the male beast, as nearly as I could see, was twice as large as the ordinary cougar, and appeared to be covered with dark round spots of great richness and beauty. His mien was erect and stately, and so majestic and proud in bearing, that it was with pleasure I contemplated him."

When John James Audubon and John Bachman were doing field work in the 1800s, Sam Houston told them he had seen jaguars "abundantly on the headwaters of some of the Rio Grande's tributaries."

The last California jaguar was killed at Palm Springs in 1860. However, jaguars continued to survive in Arizona, Texas, and New Mexico until the twentieth century. In 1920, one was seen crossing a highway three miles northwest of Tucson, Arizona. A jaguar killed in Arizona in 1971 was probably North America's last. Individual jaguars may sometimes wander from Mexico into Arizona, and a few rumors of jaguar sightings in the remote southwest have surfaced, but no confirmed reports exist.

Today the jaguar ranges through Central America to Venezuela, Brazil, and eastern Colombia, and south into Peru, Bolivia, and Argentina. It disappeared from Uruguay in 1886. However, in some of Latin America's countryside, the jaguar's hoarse cough can be heard almost nightly. Beginning with short, gutteral *uhs*, the jaguar increases them in rapidity and volume. The roar probably helps delineate a jaguar's home range and

Overleaf: Jaguars prefer to roam close to water, which they depend on for drinking and cooling off. They are excellent swimmers, island hopping easily in flooded areas or paddling wide rivers.

A small caiman makes a filling meal for this young jaguar. Adult jaguars will eat whatever is available, too, but prefer larger prey such as capybaras. They often attack by ambush, overpower with force, and kill by crushing a prey's skull with their jaws and teeth.

helps the jaguar communicate with others of its kind. How jaguars divide up space among themselves, however, remains unclear, for they seem to leave fewer visual and scent markings than other large cats do.

Jaguars live in a surprisingly wide range of habitats. When people think of jaguar habitat, many of them get an image of dense tropical rainforest. That's true, yet in Brazil, jaguars thrive in the swampy grasslands of the Pantanal. In Peru, jaguar tracks have been found at altitudes above 8,000 feet, and in northwestern Mexico, jaguars live among low scrub in fairly arid country. In general, they seem to prefer living near water. Jaguars swim well and, like the tiger, sometimes spend the heat of the day half-submerged in a stream. One was seen paddling across the broad Rio Paraguay, head and back serenely above water.

According to one Indian myth, the jaguar acquired its beautiful spotted coat by daubing mud on its body with its paws. On close inspection, the markings on a jaguar's coat do look like paw prints. Against a background color that can vary from pale gold to rich, rusty-red, the dark rosettes enclose one or two smaller spots. Along the middle of the jaguar's back, a row of black spots may merge into a solid line.

Melanistic or black jaguars are not uncommon, and at one time were regarded as a separate species. Some Indian tribes still believe these black jaguars are bigger and more ferocious than the spotted jaguars, and that the two never mingle. However, now scientists know that the black color is a recessive genetic trait, like blue eyes in humans, that follows the usual genetic rules.

From the 1940s through the 1960s, jaguar skins were in great demand. As recently as 20 years ago, 7,238 jaguar skins worth more than three-quarters of a million dollars were imported into the United States.

Since the early 1970s, the jaguar has been on the list of totally protected animals in most

While mostly loners, jaguars do interact for mating, which includes the ritual neck bite (right) during copulation. Resulting kittens barely replenish a species which is declining due to hunting and habitat destruction.

Mysteriously wearing a jaunty red tie is a ceramic jaguar (right) made by Zapotecs in Mexico between 200 B.C. and A.D. 200. It was found in an area where their kings and priests lived, one more clue to the cat's symbolic link with religion and power. The jaguar was also found on this Peruvian tapestry (below) from a later period, proving the jaguar motif spanned time and distance. Two rampant jaguars flank a stylized jaguar head.

South American countries. In Belize, a small Central American country next to the Caribbean, the world's only park dedicated to the preservation of the jaguar opened in 1984 after persistent and strenuous efforts by scientists concerned about the cat's survival. To help preserve the animal that inspired its luxury automobile, Jaguar Cars, Inc. gave $60,000 to aid the Belize preserve in planning and management. Other Latin American national parks support jaguar populations, as well. Yet these outposts are but a tiny sign of hope for the jaguar's future.

Despite the legal protection that may be on the books, jaguars are still shot. Angry ranchers understandably resent attacks on their livestock; some blame jaguars and shoot them in retaliation. As recently as 1980, biologist George Schaller was forced to abandon one of his jaguar study sites in Brazil when ranchers shot both his radio-collared jaguars.

However, studies of wild jaguars show that while jaguars do kill cattle, man sometimes contributes to the problem. Alan Rabinowitz, who spent two years studying jaguars in Belize, found that confirmed cattle-killing jaguars usually had been injured previously by shotgun wounds. He suggests that ranchers may be partially responsible for the problem when they shoot at jaguars and incapacitate them for taking their usual wild prey. Rabinowitz also found that ranchers who took care of their stock and did not allow them to wander into the forest experienced fewer losses to jaguars. Also, subsistence farmers often supplement their meager diets by hunting wild game.

A less obvious but more important threat to the jaguar's future is the elimination of its habitat. Throughout South and Central America, vast areas are being cleared for agriculture and cattle ranching. The human population, hungry for land, makes permanent dents in the ecosystem by cutting down forests and disrupting the normal hunting and traveling patterns that cats have previously established.

As more areas open up to development, the jaguar continues in direct competition with humans for its food. Turtles, tortoises, monkeys, capybara, and fish are captured and sold for their meat. Caiman populations have been decimated to satisfy the skin trade. The competition for food and living space looms as a larger threat to jaguars than the demand for their skins, and the number of jaguars is diminishing.

It is hard to envision a world without the jaguar, for even today the jaguar still plays a vital role in the lives of the people who live alongside it. The Tucaño Indians of the Amazon still believe that the roar of the jaguar is the roar of thunder, which announces the approaching rains. The jaguar is also thought by some to be the god of darkness. The spots on the jaguar's coat represented the stars in the heavens, and villagers believed the jaguar caused eclipses by swallowing the sun. Some Indian tribes still practice the custom of howling and shouting during an eclipse in an attempt to scare off the jaguar.

The Arawak Indians say that "everything has jaguar," a feeling that seems to be the root of the man-jaguar transformation rituals still performed today. It is this jaguarness that the shaman (tribal medicine man) must master, and this is why he must become a jaguar himself. By mastering the jaguar's ambivalent power, the shaman can orient the energy into channels which will prevent harm to others—or bring it on.

When a shaman transforms himself into a jaguar he "becomes" a jaguar. He eats raw meat, he sleeps on the ground, and a hallucinogenic snuff-induced trance gives him the enhanced vision and sense of smell that a jaguar is thought to have. Once transformed into a jaguar, a shaman can do good or ill. He can take revenge on an enemy, abduct a woman from a neighboring group, or cure someone of a disease.

In a sense, the person who "becomes" a jaguar is a man shorn of his cultural restrictions. His alter ego is free to act out his deepest desires and fears. Thus man borrows, for a time, the jaguar's power. Aldo Leopold described it well: "The chesty roar of jaguar in the night causes men to edge toward the blaze and draw serapes tighter. It silences the yapping dogs and starts the tethered horses milling. In announcing its mere presence in the blackness of night, the jaguar puts the animate world on edge."

Figurines made by the Olmecs (the earliest known civilization in Mexico) attest to their belief in were-jaguars, creatures with characteristics of both men and jaguars. Were-jaguars are thought to be forerunners of Aztec and Mayan rain gods and of a tribal belief in the ability of shamans (medicine men) to become jaguars for beneficial or vengeful purposes.

JAGUARUNDI

Even though the sleek jaguarundi may be the most often seen small cat in South America, its biology and behavior remain a mystery. Back in 1925, naturalist Ernest Thompson Seton noted that "a nearly clear field is offered to the young naturalist who first has a good chance to study this elegant creature." But since then, jaguarundis seldom have been studied in the wild, and the "nearly clear field" remains.

Though data on these graceful creatures remain elusive, scientists do know that the jaguarundi roams mainly during the daytime or at twilight, contrary to most other cats. That probably explains why South Americans see it more often than other wild cats.

Jaguarundis seem to prefer lowland habitats of forests or overgrown, abandoned fields, usually near streams. While they usually hunt on the ground, these cats are agile jumpers and have been observed leaping nearly six feet off the ground to swat a bird in flight.

Birds and reptiles figure largely in the jaguarundi's diet, but they also eat insects, fruit, rabbits, frogs, and fish. These cats swim well, and in some parts of Mexico they are known as otter cats because of their swimming ability. With their long slender bodies and short legs, they resemble a cross between a cat and a marten.

Jaguarundis are reputed to be quite easy to tame, and in pre-Columbian times local villagers occasionally kept them as pets to

Jaguarundis wear coats of various colors, from gray (left) to red (right). They have flat heads and long bodies and swim well—characteristics which prompt some people to liken them to otters.

Felis yagouaroundi.
Weight: 12-22 lbs.

keep down the number of mice and rats.

The jaguarundi's head is small and flattened and has short, round ears. Its short, smooth, unspotted fur shows two main color phases: blackish to brownish-gray or fox-red to bright chestnut. Kittens of both colors can be born within the same litter, somewhat like having fraternal twins, one blonde and one brunette, in the same human family. The kittens are born spotted, but the markings soon disappear. About two to four young are born.

A few jaguarundis may live in southern Arizona and Texas. In Central America and throughout much of South America as far south as Paraguay, their numbers increase.

Unlike the South American spotted cats, the jaguarundi is rarely hunted for its fur. Many historical accounts tell of the jaguarundi's reputed attraction to domestic ducks and chickens, and many jaguarundis have been shot while raiding local poultry houses. Jaguarundis also are beginning to be affected by habitat destruction, however.

OCELOT

The beauty of this big-eyed small cat may cause its downfall. The existence of the ocelot (left) is severely threatened, due mainly to demand for its pelt. About 30,000 skins were traded in 1980.

Felis pardalis.
Weight: 22-33 lbs.

Perfectly suited to a dappled world of sunlight and shadows, the ocelot is one of Latin America's most beautiful small cats. The subtle shades of its elegant coat vary so much that no two animals look alike. The ocelot's fur can be anywhere between cream and reddish grey, marked with open-centered dark spots that run in lines across its body like links in a chain. In some animals the elongate spots join together to form stripes along the body, but, unlike the tiger, ocelot stripes are horizontal rather than vertical. The dappled camouflage of the ocelot's fur allows it to blend perfectly with its forest surroundings.

Ocelots can make a living in different types of habitat as long as plenty of cover exists to hunt and hide in. Ocelots live in the dry, thick brush and chaparral of Texas, second growth forests of Central America, and undisturbed forests of South America. They are also found in seasonally flooded savannas, where they swim between outcroppings of high ground. They sometimes hunt in old fields and overgrown pastures but generally avoid open country.

Until recently the only information on the natural history and biology of the ocelot came from hunters' tales and captive animals. However, recent field studies in Texas, Belize, Venezuela, and Peru have provided some fascinating insights into the way the ocelot lives.

Though ocelots are mainly nocturnal, they also hunt during the day, especially in cloudy or rainy weather. Because ocelots are such agile climbers and leapers and frequently escape into trees when hunted, early naturalists thought that ocelots were mainly arboreal. However, recent radio tracking has revealed that ocelots hunt mostly on the ground.

Ocelots do rest in trees during the daytime, but they also find shelter in brushpiles, clumps of vines and fallen trees. Ocelots seem quite ready to take advantage of any cool, shady spot, and in Venezuela, researchers found that ocelots regularly used concrete culverts as daytime rest sites.

Both male and female ocelots maintain territories, or home ranges. Each female usually establishes her own exclusive home range, which can be as small as a third of a square mile, or as large as three square miles. Male ranges are larger and generally encompass the ranges of two or three females. Both sexes maintain their home ranges by leaving signs and scent marks in prominent places along trails. These signs seem to act as "occupied" signals, informing other ocelots that the area is spoken for.

Ocelots cross and recross their home ranges in search of prey. One researcher found that ocelots crossed their entire range every two to four days.

Though all successful attacks depend upon surprise, ocelots probably use different methods for hunting different types of prey. When hunting rabbits, the ocelot may choose a likely spot and wait in silent ambush for an hour or more. But when hunting mice and rats, it usually walks quietly along a trail, listening for rustles or other signs of rodent activity. On full-moon nights, ocelots often spend less time moving along roads and trails, and confine their hunting to dense, brushy areas.

Ocelots catch whatever is most abundant, and their diet usually changes with the seasons. They generally feed on animals weighing less than two pounds, such as opossums, mice, rats, and rabbits. However, they also eat snakes, lizards, insects, land crabs, and fish. In Peru's Manu, ocelots glut themselves with fish spawning in shallow streams. One ocelot was described as "resting with his belly so distended that he was reluctant to move."

Like most cats, ocelots are solitary hunters. However, while traveling around their ranges, neighbors probably encounter one another and may spend time together.

Ocelots hunt for prey mostly on the ground but also climb and swim adeptly. They will kill whatever is available and possible to subdue, including lizards, turtles, and spiny rats.

Territorial males undoubtedly cross paths with the females in their range. Unless the female is in heat, these meetings are brief.

While mating, a pair may stay together for a day or two, but afterward each returns to his or her own lifestyle.

A female ocelot raises her young without help from the male. After a 70-day gestation period she gives birth to usually only one or two kittens. The well-protected den is usually in a dense thicket or among the roots of a fallen tree, and the young remain in and around the den for several weeks. During the daytime, while the female rests nearby, the ocelot kittens pounce and play, practicing for the time when they will have to hunt for themselves. However, ocelot mothers do not rest for long. One researcher's records show that an ocelot mother's activity doubled as she hunted for herself and her brood or checked out her territory.

Young ocelots remain dependent on their mother for meals for several months, but when they are about two months old the mother begins to take them on hunting trips. When they can hunt for themselves they use their mother's territory until they become sexually mature at about a year and a half of age. Then the young ocelots must travel in search of an unoccupied territory. At this stage of their lives they are particularly vulnerable, and many young die before they have a chance to breed. When they live near human populations they are often killed crossing roads or raiding poultry houses.

Where they are allowed to, ocelots can coexist with humans. While they do well in secondary forests, however, other parts of their range are being chopped away by habitat destruction.

The ocelot lives throughout much of Central and South America, including Colombia, Venezuela, Bolivia, Paraguay, Brazil, northern Argentina, and Peru. A few live in Arizona and Texas, marking the cat's northernmost boundaries.

The ocelot is frequently hunted, and international demand for its beautiful skin has depleted the ocelot population. Ocelots are small, and because no two are alike, it takes about twelve pelts to make a coat. Thus the fur trade requires an enormous number of skins. In 1980 in West Germany, ocelot coats were selling for as much as $40,000.

In 1972, importation of ocelot skins to the United States was prohibited. Many Latin American countries have since passed laws to protect their spotted cats, and the trade in their skins is partially regulated by the Convention on International Trade in Endangered Species (CITES). Despite this protection, at first ocelot skins continued to be traded on world fur markets—31,000 ocelot skins as recently as 1980. Now, the animals have either been depleted through hunting, or CITES has had a significant effect, for in 1984, only 4,000 or so ocelot skins were traded. While ocelots are still common in Peru, they are considered threatened throughout much of the rest of their range.

OCELOT AND JAGUARUNDI IN NORTH AMERICA

While greater numbers live in Latin America, the ocelot and the jaguarundi (see page 72) have managed to retain a toehold in the United States, according to a young Texas researcher, Michael Tewes, of the Wildlife Research Institute. Since 1981, Tewes and Daniel Navarro have scoured the brushy country of southwestern Texas, observing signs of 80 to 120 of the spotted cats.

Until the twentieth century, ocelots also lived in Arizona, Louisiana, and Arkansas. In these states, hunting and severe habitat loss sealed the ocelot's fate.

Although the jaguarundi's coat hasn't appealed to the fur trade, its habitat has fallen prey to development. Consequently, its numbers have dwindled in almost all of the United States.

MARGAY

A margay (left) may look like an ocelot, but differences set them apart, such as the margay's slimmer build, smaller size, and longer tail. Agile climbers, margays owe their skill to their flexible ankles and soft, wide feet. Margays have been known to hang by their feet from branches.

Felis wiedii.
Weight: 6-11 lbs.

While most other cats back down a tree hind feet first, the agile, acrobatic margay can boldly scamper down head first. The margay spends much of its time in the trees, and its climbing ability is legendary. It can spring out of trees, drop from branch to branch, or dangle from its hind feet like a trapeze artist.

Captive margays have been seen jumping nearly eight feet straight in the air and twelve feet horizontally. A scientist who kept two margays as pets described them as "climbing like monkeys." He reported that even during a fall, they had such fast reactions that they were able to grab hold of a branch or vine with one paw and climb up again.

Margays have several anatomical adaptations that help them perform these astonishing acrobatic feats. Their flexible ankles can rotate 180 degrees outward, which allows them to get a firm hold on anything they climb. Instead of the narrow, rather firm foot of the house cat, margays have broad, soft feet with very mobile toes. This gives them a more effective grip for precision balancing and jumping.

The margay looks like a junior version of the ocelot. In many parts of Latin America, the natives do not distinguish between the two, or refer to the margay as the "little ocelot." The margay is smaller and more slimly built than the ocelot, however, and has a relatively longer tail.

One of the most striking differences between the margay and the ocelot is fur texture. Ocelots have sleek, short-haired coats, while margay fur is thick, soft, and longer than that of many other spotted cats.

The margay's coat is golden brown, with white on the belly, chest, throat, and chin. The spots are either solid black or have paler centers and are arranged in vertical rows along the body. The backs of the ears are black with white central spots, and the tail is marked with spots or rings.

Though in some places it lives alongside its larger cousin, the margay seems to be more specific in its habitat requirements than the ocelot. Margays live almost exclusively in humid evergreen forests, but sometimes are found in coffee or cocoa plantations.

Almost nothing is known of the natural behavior of this agile little cat. One scientist working in Belize managed to capture and radio-collar a single animal, but this has been the only study of margays in the wild.

The radio-collared margay was found to be strictly nocturnal, most active between one and five in the morning. During the daytime it rested in a tangle of liana vines or the bole of a palm tree, always at least 20 feet off the ground. Most of the radio-collared margay's diet consisted of small, tree-living rodents, but it also ate opossums, birds, insects, and fruit. Elsewhere, margays have been found to eat squirrels, sloths, capuchin monkeys, and porcupines.

Unlike most other small cats, margays usually give birth to only one or two kittens at a time. The kittens open their eyes at about two weeks of age and are weaned at two months of age.

Margays are threatened by the same pressures that face all the small spotted cats, namely hunting and loss of habitat. Like ocelots, margays are hunted for their beautiful fur. Their fur is worth only about a fourth of what the ocelot's is, however, and many margays are caught by accident in traps intended for ocelots. Hunters sometimes cut margays' tails short to try to fool buyers into thinking they are getting ocelot skins.

Mexico is the northernmost limit of the margay's distribution. From Panama, northern Colombia and Peru, the margay ranges to northern and eastern Paraguay, northern Uruguay and northern Argentina.

Despite the fact that the margay is listed as an endangered species and international agreements such as CITES restrict its trade, more than 20,000 skins of this beautiful spotted cat were sold on the world market in 1980 alone.

PAMPAS CAT
& Other Little-Known Cats

The pampas cat (left) is named after one of its habitats—the grass plains, or "pampas," of South America. Little is known about these long-haired cats and it is rarely even possible to observe them in zoos.

PAMPAS CAT
Felis colocolo. *Weight: 7-14 lbs.*

In the Andes, this small feline lives at high altitudes; in Argentina it roams open grasslands; and in Chile it ranges through cloud forests. The pampas cat seems able to live at almost any high altitude, yet little else is known about its biology or habits. It is thought to be nocturnal and to feed on small rodents and ground-nesting birds.

The pampas cat looks like a heavy-set housecat. It has a small head, rather broad face, and pointed ears. When the cat is frightened or nervous, the long, mane-like hairs on its back stand erect, giving the cat a larger and more formidable appearance.

The color, pattern, and even texture of the coat varies from one pampas cat to the next. Some are dark with red-grey spots or streaks, while others are almost unpatterned, except for brown bands on the legs and tail. Depending on where the cat lives, its coat can feel thick and soft or thin and strawlike.

The backs of the ears are black with a central white spot, a characteristic shared by several other small cats and by tigers and lions. While no one knows for sure why the spots are there, scientists have suggested that they may serve as markers to help young cats follow their mother.

The pampas cat is found mainly in Ecuador, Peru, Brazil, Chile, Paraguay, Argentina, and Uruguay. Few are in zoos.

MOUNTAIN CAT
Felis jacobita. *Weight: 7-15 lbs.*

The mountain cat was first described in 1865, but it was 1980 before scientists caught more than a glimpse of this little-known cat in the wild. In that year two Argentinians managed to watch and photograph a mountain cat for two hours. When they first saw the animal it was approaching a stream to drink. It did not seem to be bothered by their presence, so they followed as the cat strolled along a nearby lake, observed warily by a flock of ducks. The ducks did not flee, probably because they could keep the cat—which usually stalks by stealth—in sight. Later, the cat stopped for a 20-minute nap beneath a rock overhang, but it was disturbed by a bird's alarm calls and wandered out of sight.

It seems unbelievable, but these observations provided the only information scientists have been able to gather about the mountain cat's behavior in the wild. The scientists, G. J. Scrocchi and S. P. Halloy, had done field work in the area 33 times over 12 years, but only spotted the mountain cat this one time. That gives an idea of the cat's scarcity, and also of its ability to conceal itself among vegetation or rocks.

The typical haunts of the mountain cat may be partially responsible for the lack of information. It appears to be a high altitude animal; so far, it has been reported only on barren slopes above 11,500 feet in the Andes of Chile, Peru, Bolivia, and Argentina. The cat's silvery fur, striped with brown, blends perfectly with its rocky surroundings.

LITTLE SPOTTED CAT
Felis tigrina. *Weight: 4-6 lbs.*

About half the size of an ordinary house cat, the little spotted cat is just big enough to be regularly hunted for its fur. In 1980, about 33,500 skins were traded on the world fur market. That year, the little spotted cat, also known as the tiger cat, was put on the list of endangered species, yet it continues to lose ground to poaching and habitat destruction.

Like the acrobatic margay, the little spotted cat is an agile climber and leaper. Its tail, which is nearly 40 percent of its overall length, helps it balance during leaps and swerves. A forest-dweller, it probably feeds on lizards, mice, and birds such as the large-footed finch.

Little-spotted cats live from Costa Rica south through Venezuela, Brazil, Colombia, and Ecuador, but they are not abundant anywhere in their range.

Although similar in appearance, Geoffroy's cat (right) and the kodkod face different threats from humans. The kodkod's small size saves it from the fur trade, but its forest home makes it a victim of habitat destruction. Geoffroy's cat, which lives in rocky terrain, is larger than the kodkod, and its soft pelt is one of the most traded in the world.

GEOFFROY'S CAT
Felis geoffroyi. *Weight: 4-7 lbs.*

After the bobcat, the Geoffroy's cat is the world's most frequently hunted cat, at least according to records of fur traders. In 1980, 145,000 Geoffroy's cat skins were traded worldwide, according to TRAFFIC, USA, a World Wildlife Fund project.

Furriers and buyers prize the fur of this housecat-sized felid because of its exotic colors of its coat and the elegant markings.

In 1984, about 22,000 skins were traded on the world market, according to TRAFFIC, USA, a monitoring program of the World Wildlife Fund. It isn't yet known if this figure resulted from enforcement through CITES, an international treaty, or because of scarcity from overhunting.

Some Geoffroy's cat furs are smoky-grey and others are lion-like ochre, with every imaginable color in between. Small black spots cover the animal's body and legs, and two black streaks run down each cheek. Geoffroy's cat is roughly the same size as the margay, but it looks more robust and has a shorter tail. The tail is spotted at the base and ringed toward the tip.

The cat was named after Geoffroy St. Hilaire, a French naturalist, and once was thought to be the same species as the kodkod, which it resembles. Zoologists later classified them separately.

In keeping with its local name of "gato montes," or mountain cat, Geoffroy's cat lives mainly in rocky, shrub-covered terrain. It prefers foothills to steep mountains, however, and is also seen in open woodlands, brushy areas, savannas, and marshes.

Most Geoffroy's cats roam in the Bolivian Andes, Uruguay, southern Brazil, Paraguay, Chile, and part of Argentina. Paraguay and Bolivia have banned trade in the skins of this cat because further trade could doom it to extinction.

Even though Geoffroy's cats have often been captured by fur trappers, scientists know almost nothing about the cat's habits in the wild. So far, researchers have published data on only one radio-collared cat in Paraguay, which had a home range of little more than a square mile. Biologists in Chile have put radio-collars on four cats, and in mid-1987, are still observing them and collecting data.

The cat is thought to be nocturnal, although it is sometimes seen at twilight. It has been sighted sleeping in trees during the day. Geoffroy's cats are reported to feed on rats, birds, wild guinea pigs, and agoutis.

KODKOD
Felis guigna. *Weight: 4-5 lbs.*

This oddly named cat is the smallest wild cat in the western hemisphere. So few observations have been made of the kodkod's behavior in the wild that cat experts do not even know whether it hunts by day or night. Even captive kodkods are hard to come by —not a single North American zoo can claim a kodkod.

This almost unknown cat is believed to live in forests, but experts disagree on whether it hunts on the ground or in trees. Some researchers say the kodkod climbs well and easily, and it is thought to eat rats, mice, and birds. No data are available, however, on the biology, behavior and reproductive habits of this tiny cat.

The kodkod is greyish-brown with round blackish spots on its back and flanks. The tail is ringed with narrow black bands, and the backs of its ears are black with white central spots. Like its larger relative the jaguar, melanistic (black-coated) kodkods have occasionally been seen.

The kodkod appears to be confined to a relatively small area in Chile and Argentina, where it is totally protected by law. Populations throughout its range are thought to be decreasing, however, because of habitat destruction. Because the kodkod is so small, it is not often hunted for its pelt.

ASIA AND EUROPE

BY PETER JACKSON

TIGER

Largest feline on earth, the tiger (left) exudes grace, beauty, and awesome strength. The markings on a tiger's forehead serve as its "fingerprint"—while similar, no two are exactly alike, and alert human observers can identify a certain tiger by its facial stripes.

Panthera tigris. *Weight: females 163-370 lbs. males 400-600 lbs.*

The tiger lay down about 100 yards ahead and gazed at me. After a while it stood up, scent marked a nearby tree and edged forward, until, about 25 yards away, it turned into the bushes. I could just make out the tip of the tiger's ear and the curve of its head, and saw it looking at me curiously before continuing on its way.

As it disappeared I pondered the irony: the tiger, reduced so greatly in numbers and distribution, now stands on the verge of extinction—just when its true nature is being understood and humans are appreciating the intricate relationships of animals and their habitat.

All told, a reasonable estimate of the number of tigers alive today is 7,000 to 8,000. At least half of these tigers are gravely threatened, and even the well-guarded Indian tiger will survive only if we humans are willing to make the continued effort.

Why should we? The world would be a poorer place without these creatures, which represent the very spirit of the wild. The great cat has always impressed itself on human consciousness, symbolizing power, authority, courage, and ferocity. Shakespeare's Henry V encouraged his men fighting the French at Agincourt:

> . . . when the blast of war blows in
>   our ears,
> Then imitate the action of the tiger:
> Stiffen the sinews, summon up
>   the blood,
> Disguise fair nature with
>   hard-favoured rage.

To poet William Blake, the tiger was a powerful symbol, combining both good and evil. He celebrated the tiger in the words:

> Tyger! Tyger! burning bright
> In the forests of the night.
> What immortal hand or eye
> Dare frame thy fearful symmetry.

Englishmen such as Shakespeare and Blake admired the tiger from a distance, but for the people of Asia the tiger has been a living presence and a powerful symbol in their lives. Chinese see the markings on the tiger's forehead as the character Wang, meaning King, and Chinese ambassadors once carried a Tiger Stick as a mark of authority.

The tiger has been a popular theme of Chinese art in scrolls and temple paintings, and when the Year of the Tiger returns every twelfth year, Chinese children get tiger hats, shoes, and gifts to bring good luck.

Tipu Sultan (see carved tiger, page 89) of India was so enamored of the tiger that he had a tiger throne; his weapons, clothes and even his handkerchiefs bore a tiger stripe.

In India the female deity Durga is depicted riding a tiger. In Bengal, woodcutters, honey collectors, and fishermen entering the realm of notorious man-eating tigers in the mangrove forests of the Sundarbans region still pray for protection at shrines dedicated to Banbibi and Shahjungli (the goddess and god of the jungle) and Dakshin Roy (the legendary tiger deity).

The lingering legend of the man-eating tigers perhaps sticks in the human mind more than any other stories of the great cats of the world. But how much is fact and how much fiction?

Of course, many man-eating tigers have prowled the forests just as man-eating lions and leopards have, but in most cases, they have done so because they had earlier been disabled by injury or age and were unable to capture their normal prey. The tigers in the jungles of Asia are not all ferocious man-eaters as so often depicted.

The famous British hunter Jim Corbett, who spent a lifetime trekking through India's forests, once described the great cat as "a large-hearted gentleman."

Try telling that to modern-day Sundarbans residents. They regard their chances of becoming a tiger statistic in somewhat the

Known to Europeans mainly through the tales of travelers, the tiger became the subject of legends. One, depicted in a medieval English manuscript (below), describes how to steal cubs. Mirrors dropped along the escape route would supposedly distract the mother tiger while she stopped to look at her reflection, thus allowing the kidnapper to get away.

The tiger's power has triggered the imagination and respect of Asian people for centuries. A Ming dynasty silk painting (right) depicts a tiger and a dragon, symbols usually representing the two great forces of nature.

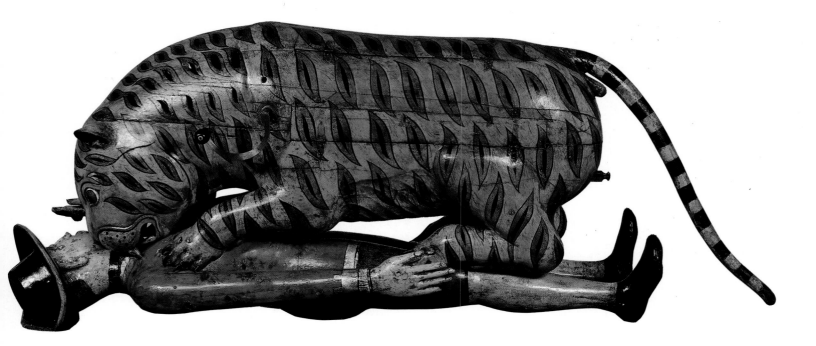

same way Americans look at their chances of becoming a car accident victim on the way to work—while not likely, it *is* possible, and so a fact of life.

While about 30 people were killed by tigers in India in 1986, humans are not normal prey, and the pattern of a tiger's daily life hardly includes hunting humans.

In late afternoon the tiger rises from its rest and starts in search of prey. During its patrol the tiger usually follows game trails, even using manmade roads, alert for prey. If it spots likely prey, it begins to stalk, crouched low, eyes intent, until it has moved into position for the mighty bound. Grabbing the prey with its forepaws, the tiger crashes to the ground, keeping well clear of its prey's thrashing hooves and horns.

If it kills, the tiger does not begin to eat right away. Instead it drags the carcass to a secluded place where it will feed during the night, breaking away from time to time to drink. Usually it remains close to the kill, defending its prize from vultures, hyenas, jackals, and other scavengers. Depending on its size, the prey may last the cat for several days. If the tiger leaves the kill, it covers it with leaves and branches.

A tiger may be successful in killing only once in several attempts. Humans rarely witness a tiger kill, and the eminent wildlife biologist George Schaller saw only one attack during a two-year study in India. Corbett saw only twenty in half a century.

In recent years one tiger achieved fame by hunting openly in India's Ranthambhore reserve. Named Ghengis Khan because of the ruthless speed with which he drove other tigers from his chosen range, this tiger stalked sambar deer grazing in shallow lakes.

The wooden effigy of Tipu's Tiger (above) depicts a Bengal tiger devouring an Englishman. An organ inside the tiger produces shrieks of the person in distress. The piece was made for Tipu Sultan, an Indian ruler in the 1700s who was obsessed with tigers as well as his hatred for the British.

The pattern of the tiger's stripes enables the stealthy cat to blend with the shadows of the forest and grasslands (below) as it stalks prey. Head tucked low,   *the hungry tiger (right) edges as close to the unwary prey as possible, patiently waiting until just the right moment to leap from the grass.*

He was frequently observed as he made spectacular dashes into the water to grab one of the less fleet. He later disappeared, but other tigers had noted his successful technique and began to copy it.

While deer and pig are favored prey, providing ample food for several days, the tiger will also eat many small animals, including monkeys, porcupines, rodents, pangolins, reptiles, fish, crabs—in fact, almost anything edible that moves. Immensely powerful jaw muscles make the tiger's canine teeth deadly weapons that can crunch the vertebrae of even large prey. The rear teeth crush bones and shear off lumps of meat, which are swallowed whole.

Living a precarious life of feast or famine, the tiger fills its belly whenever it has an opportunity. After glutting himself, a male can appear heavily pregnant. The gorging is understandable, for it may be days before the cat can kill large prey again.

Tigers usually hunt alone, though they do socialize, and lion-like "prides" consisting of females and cubs and (probably related) mature males have been seen in Ranthambhore, India. Observers even saw signs of cooperative hunting in the grasslands around the lakes, although the groups were probably families hunting together.

Usually, however, the tigress and her cubs form the principal social unit, with the male present only for mating. The male tiger is attracted by the female's scent marks, which indicate that she is ready to mate, and by her frequent calls.

Water sprays wildly as a tiger splashes after a sambar, one of its favorite prey. The tiger will try to drag its victim down, then seize its throat in a strangling grip.

The female flirts with him, rubbing her face and body against his and then distancing herself and rolling on the ground. After some time she crouches, haunches raised and tail pulled aside. The male straddles her, usually grabbing the loose skin of her nape in his jaws. Growls and squeals accompany the short copulation until, after the climax, the tigress swings round and lashes at her mate, who leaps clear.

The sequence is repeated at intervals of about 20 minutes for several hours. Repeated copulations over two or three days may be necessary to induce ovulation, although this has not been scientifically proven.

Gestation lasts around 100 days before the cubs are born, blind and helpless. By the tenth day the eyes open and soon afterward milk teeth appear. Cubs begin to eat meat after about two months, but continue to suckle until about six months old. The tigress may give birth to four cubs (up to seven have been recorded), but usually only one or two survive. Scientist George Schaller speculates that hyenas or jackals may prey on the young when the mother goes hunting. Several accounts also detail male tigers killing cubs.

The cubs that do survive spend the next few months learning the techniques of stalking, attacking, and killing. The lessons start early, with small cubs "hunting" their mother's flicking tail, and continue as she takes them with her, sometimes disabling a prey animal and leaving it for the cubs to practice the actual killing.

At around 18 months the cubs, now almost fully grown, drift away from the mother. She may even drive them off when she feels the urge to mate again. Now the cubs enter one of the most dangerous phases of their lives—finding a home range. For the females this means an area within the range of a male, with enough prey, cover, and water to raise cubs. Studies in Nepal's Royal Chitwan National Park showed that a tigress' female cub could sometimes establish

After killing its prey (right), a tiger eats until it can eat no more (below). Scientists say a female tiger in the wild was seen gorging 66 pounds of meat —one fifth of her body weight. Its shoulders and back ripple with steely muscles as the tiger drinks (far right).

herself in her mother's territory and later breed there.

But the young males face a battle with powerful, mature tigers for a place to live. Young males may be forced to the edges of reserves, where wild prey is scarce but livestock is available. There they may take cattle, and risk poisoning by irate graziers. They might even attack and kill humans, probably by accident the first time.

One day in Chitwan Park news reached our camp that a tiger had killed a local villager. It was easy to reconstruct the encounter. The tiger had come up a river bank and been confronted by the village schoolteacher on his way for his morning bath. The startled tiger leapt on the equally startled man and killed him with a bite on the head. Then it ran and hid. Because it had been radio-collared it was quickly caught; it died later in captivity.

The young tiger had been crippled in a fight with another male, and, unable to catch normal prey, it had settled near villages where it fed on scrub cattle. The tiger was no

man-eater, although it might have become one under the circumstances. Its short life illustrates the hazards facing a young tiger.

More fortunate young males may be able to wrest a territory from another tiger and take over any breeding females. One powerful tiger in Chitwan had seven females in his huge range, which was delineated in usual tiger fashion by scent sprays of urine and secretions on rocks, trees, and bushes; scratches on trees and scrapes on the ground; and prominent piles of feces to warn other tigers of his dominant presence. Even though a tiger may claim a large area, it concentrates on an area where prey is abundant.

Tigers were plentiful in the past when forests and grasslands with flourishing wildlife covered vast areas in Asia. Fossil remains suggest that the tiger evolved in Siberia, some having been found as far north as the edge of the Arctic Ocean, far from the tropical areas with which it is associated today. Tigers still roam in icy, snowbound forests in temperatures of -40°C in the far

Lounging and playing in marshes and rivers, tigers seek relief from the overpowering heat.

eastern USSR and northeast China. With thick fur and a deep layer of insulating fat, the Siberian tiger is the largest of the tigers, exceeding 10 feet in length and sometimes weighing more than 700 pounds. Some have measured up to 13 feet.

From Siberia tigers spread to the tropical lands of southern Asia and to the Indian sub-continent. Another arm of tiger expansion passed north of the Tibetan plateau to the Caspian region and eastern Turkey.

Yet by the close of the nineteenth century, the range and numbers of tigers were dwindling. British soldiers and officials, as well as Indian princes, accounted for killing hundreds of them. The Maharajah of Surguja claimed to have shot 1,150.

Hunters made exaggerated claims for the size of their trophies. Measurements were made over the curves of the tiger's back from the tip of the nose to the tail, which gave a more impressive length than the straight line "between pegs" set at either end. Stories were even told of tapes marked in 11-inch feet to boost measurements.

By the 1930s many experts thought tiger numbers were diminishing, and Jim Corbett and others predicted extinction unless hunting was restrained.

World War II accelerated the destruction of forests because timber was in great demand. In the next two decades, rapidly growing cities and villages pressed deeper and deeper into tiger domain. Protection of the private hunting preserves of maharajas collapsed after India gained its independence in 1947. Night hunting with jeeps and spot-

Its long-haired winter coat helps insulate a Siberian tiger (left). The rare cat's beautiful fur also has encouraged poaching, however, and only a few dozen Siberian tigers remain. Young adults tussle (above), their combative spirit preparing them for a life of hunting.

Overleaf: *A dutiful young tiger follows its mother as she veers into the underbrush. Some scientists speculate that the white spots on the mother's ears serve as markers for cubs to follow. By the end of their second year, young tigers begin to break their family ties, having already learned to hunt on their own.*

lights became widespread, leading to mass slaughter of all large mammals, the tiger's prey as well as the tiger itself. The chemical DDT was used to clear malaria-ridden areas that were wildlife sanctuaries. To expand agriculture, rural people destroyed tigers by inserting pesticides in their kills. With prices for skins soaring, the slaughter grew.

Elsewhere in Asia the tiger was also rapidly losing its habitat. The South China tiger was declared a pest and teams of hunters went after it to claim rewards. The Javan tiger followed the Bali subspecies into extinction, and the Sumatran tiger declined rapidly despite legal protection.

The tide of destruction was stemmed to a large extent by Operation Tiger, the campaign launched by the World Wildlife Fund (WWF) and the International Union for Conservation of Nature and Natural Resources (IUCN) in the early 1970s. Dynamic support for the campaign came from the late Indira Gandhi, prime minister of India, and from the Royal Family of Nepal.

With political and financial support, conservationists in India and Nepal strengthened the laws against poaching and either purchased or caused to be set aside the protected land that has brought about the relatively healthy situation of the Indian tiger today. Fifteen years ago only about 2,500 tigers remained in India, Nepal, Bangladesh, and Bhutan. Today as many as 5,000 may roam there.

Forests in southeast Asia may still hold more than 2,000 Indo-Chinese tigers, but the Sumatran tiger is rapidly losing habitat to human settlement and may number fewer than 1,000.

The Siberian tiger population in the Soviet Union is reported to be stable at about 300 cats, but only 50 or so scattered animals survive in northeast China, still hunted for their skins, and especially for bones to make medicine. With the South China tiger similarly threatened, some Chinese specialists predict that the country may no longer have tigers by the turn of the century.

In a peculiar grimace known as flehmen, *the tiger (left) exposes a sensitive organ in its mouth which can detect scents of other tigers. Surveying its domain, the powerful tiger (right) seems less forbidding from this vantage point.*

JUNGLE CAT

One of Asia's most common wild cats, the jungle cat is agile enough to catch birds with a well-timed leap. Also known as the reed cat, it roams secluded banks of rivers.

Felis chaus. *Weight: 9-30 lbs.*

In rural India a common wild cat, which sometimes raids the chicken runs, is the jungle cat, an animal somewhat larger than a domestic cat and with markedly long legs and a short tail. The jungle cat was well known to the ancient Egyptians, who in their wall paintings depicted it hunting small birds and mammals.

Active in daylight as well as at night, the jungle cat's favorite prey is hares. The cat needs to make a quick kill, for hares are agile at twisting and turning and thus have a good chance of escaping. Jungle cats also eat rodents, lizards, snakes, frogs, and birds and have been known to kill young fawns. Flying birds may be caught by a great leap and a swift blow of the paw, which knocks them down. One scientist working in Soviet Tadzhikistan found a jungle cat eating olives.

Jungle cats sometimes make dens in old burrows of badgers, porcupines, and foxes. Their courtship call is like that of a domestic cat, but deeper in tone and louder. After a gestation period of about 56 days, three to four cubs are born, which can be tamed easily, although they react savagely if interfered with at feeding time.

The jungle cat ranges from Egypt through the Middle East, Central Asia, and the Indian subcontinent. Because it is often found in tall reed beds around river banks, it is also known as the reed cat.

Its ears are tipped with black tufts, reminiscent of the lynx. The coat varies from yellowish grey to brown and tawny red, with black varieties living in some areas. Some jungle cats have stripes on the upper parts of their legs, and all of them have a ringed tail with a black tip. Black stripes present at birth disappear as the kittens grow.

CLOUDED LEOPARD

Among the most beautiful of cats, the graceful clouded leopard climbs and leaps with ease. Its three-foot tail is about half of the cat's total body length. Humans rarely see it in the wild, however. It daily grows more vulnerable to extinction as its forest habitat is cleared away for farms.

Neofelis nebulosa.
Weight: 35-50 lbs.

In the rain forests of tropical Asia a miniature version of the sabertooth tiger hunts deer, monkeys, and pigs, killing them with its long, sharp canines. This is the clouded leopard, among the most beautifully patterned of the cats. Its spots remind the Chinese of mint leaves and they call it the "mint leopard." For Malaysians it is the "tree tiger" because it is often seen resting in the branches of the jungle.

In fact, the clouded leopard, with its long canine teeth, is no more related to the extinct sabertooths than other cats are, for the prehistoric great cat was the end of an evolutionary line. Yet the clouded leopard is distinct from others of the cat family and stands alone in its own genus as *Neofelis nebulosa*, literally the new cat with a cloudy pelt.

Averaging about six feet in length, including a three-foot tail, the clouded leopard has characteristics of both the big cats and the small ones. It purrs like small cats, for instance. The clouded leopard has webbed toes and double claw sheaths.

Sir Stamford Raffles, the founder of Singapore, obtained a specimen from Sumatra in the late eighteenth century, and clouded leopards were subsequently found to live in the region from eastern Nepal through northeast India, southeast Asia, southern China, Taiwan, and Borneo.

Because the cats were frequently seen in trees, the clouded leopard once was widely thought to be arboreal. Even now, little is known about its way of life, but some scientists now consider it basically a terrestrial animal which merely rests in trees, possibly to escape the leeches which infest humid forests.

In Borneo the clouded leopard is the top predator, and it is reported to feed on pigs, deer, monkeys, orangutans, and rodents. In Sarawak, the Malaysian state on the north coast, scientists found that a clouded leopard had paddled through mangroves, possibly in pursuit of pigs swimming to an island. Pet clouded leopards have been seen plucking chickens and licking off fur before eating monkey meat, just as most cats do.

In other parts of its range the clouded leopard has to compete with the more powerful leopard and tiger, and it is thought that, for its own protection, it might be more arboreal in these regions than in Borneo.

Being an inhabitant of primary forest, its numbers must be declining as the forest is cleared. The status of the clouded leopard is virtually unknown, but it is classed as "vulnerable" by IUCN (International Union for Conservation of Nature). It is rare in Taiwan, but some may survive in the mountains.

SNOW LEOPARD

In the high mountains of Asia a ghostly figure sits among the crags, its greenish eyes intently surveying the panorama. The snow leopard, its greyish-white coat dappled with black spots and rosettes, blends easily into the landscape of rocks and snow as it hunts wild sheep and goats, marmots and smaller creatures.

Information about the life of the snow leopard came almost entirely from hunters until scientist Rodney Jackson began studies in the remote Langu valley in Nepal a few years ago. He trapped and radio-collared five animals, which he tracked for two years.

Jackson found that the radio-collared snow leopards were mainly active in the early morning and twilight hours. They preferred to move along major ridgelines, edges of bluffs, and bases of cliffs. The home ranges, which overlapped, varied from 4 to 15 square miles, but this does not take into account the enormous vertical distances of the mountains involved. The cats seemed to prefer the places where mountain streams came together—also the haunt of numbers of blue sheep, reportedly a favorite prey.

Jackson's colleague, Gary Ahlborn, noted snow leopards marking with scrapes, feces, scent-spraying, and claw-raking, especially at prominent locations with an unobstructed view. He surmised that snow leopards do this to minimize encounters with other cats in shared home ranges.

Snow leopards follow the migrations of prey, yet when traditional prey are scarce (and when livestock are available), cattle inevitably fall victim. Livestock owners have struck back by trapping and poisoning the cats. Like other predators, snow leopards can be overstimulated into an orgy of killing when attacking prey such as goats in a restricted space. This reaction seems to have a biological cause, so wildlife managers hope to prevent the chain reaction from ever starting in the first place. They are recommending better protection of penned animals.

Biologist George Schaller, who was the first to photograph snow leopards, gave this account of the hunting snow leopard: "She advanced slowly down the slope . . . carefully placing each paw until she reached a boulder above the goat . . . then leaped to the ground. When the goat turned to flee, she lunged and with a snap clamped her teeth on its throat . . . and grabbed the goat's shoulders with her massive paws."

The snow leopard, slightly smaller than the average common leopard, is about seven feet long, including a bushy three-foot tail. Its dense, rather woolly fur protects it from the severe cold. Extremely agile, as it must be in its rugged homeland, snow leopards are excellent leapers. One was reported to have jumped 45 feet over a ditch.

Given the harsh environment in which it lives and the sparse amount of prey, the snow leopard has probably never been common. Because of the depredations resulting from the trade in its beautiful pelt, it has long been considered in danger of extinction. However, recent information suggests about 6,000 to 7,000 could still exist, more than commonly thought. They are spread over a huge arc from Mongolia and China through the USSR, Afghanistan, Pakistan, India, Nepal, and Bhutan and are by no means safe from the threat of extinction.

Joint surveys by the Wildlife Institute of India and the International Snow Leopard Trust of Seattle, Washington, as well as by a British biologist, have found signs of relatively good snow leopard populations in the western Himalayas. Soviet scientists have estimated that about 2,000 snow leopards live in Kirghizia (USSR)—where they have been seen resting in vulture nests built low to the ground. Many snow leopards seen in zoos come from Kirghizia.

Estimates by Mongolian and Polish specialists, who believe 2,000 to 4,000 snow leopards live in the western Mongolian mountains, are considered too high by many other experts. Nevertheless, a trophy hunting program permits foreign hunters to shoot five snow leopards known to be predators of livestock. High hunting fees go mainly to reimburse the livestock owners.

The fur has been in demand, and one recent visitor reported that snow leopard coats were for sale in the tourist shops of China. Buyers face confiscation of such coats by their home authorities, however, under an international convention to control trade. The cat also is poached for bones and other parts for medicinal use, especially since the preferred tiger bones are now very scarce.

The future of the snow leopard depends on adequate, well-policed reserves with sufficient prey and on efficient enforcement of the snow leopard's protected status. Like the tiger in the forest, the snow leopard is an evocative symbol of the wild. Schaller summed it up well: "When the last snow leopard has stalked among the crags, a spark of life will have gone, turning the mountains into stones of silence."

The beautiful and ghostly snow leopard has inspired poems and paintings, entranced humans worldwide, and defied study by all but the most patient of scientists. About seven feet long, including a bushy three-foot tail, the snow leopard is covered by dense, wooly fur to protect it from harsh winters.

Panthera uncia. *Weight: 88-165 lbs.*

FISHING CAT

Like a housecat catching goldfish in a bowl, the fishing cat sits on a rock and flips its unsuspecting prey from the water onto the land, where it eats it. The fishing cat, however, is larger and much more powerful than a domestic cat—so powerful, in fact, that one was able to kill a leopard twice its size. On another occasion, a fishing cat turned on pursuing dogs, breaking the jaw of one with a blow, grasping a second by the neck and throwing it to the ground, and then making off with a third. An eagle was also attacked and killed by a fishing cat. Other cats are said to have killed calves and sheep.

Although the fishing cat has been found up to 5,000 feet in the Himalayas, it generally frequents marshes, swamps, and streams. Despite its name, it once had the reputation of not caring much for entering water. Since then, however, it has been seen wading and swimming. Biologist T. J. Roberts reported that in Pakistan a fishing cat swam under water down a narrow channel to escape from dogs. It propelled itself with its powerful, partially-webbed hind feet and appeared to keep its eyes open. Observers also say it swims under water and grabs unsuspecting ducks from below.

The fishing cat probably once lived throughout large parts of the Indian subcontinent. Now only a relict population exists on the southwest coast and in Sri Lanka. It also lives in Sumatra and Java.

The fishing cat is a handsome animal, generally grizzled grey with vertical rows of dark spots that run across the crown and along the neck. Its head is broad and its black-ringed tail is relatively short, being only about one-third the length of the body. Apart from having webs between its toes, the fishing cat has claws that do not retract fully into the sheaths.

Some zoos, including ones in Philadelphia and Frankfurt, have successfully bred fishing cats. Two or three cubs were born, fully furred and clawed.

A fishing cat scoops persistently in shallow water, searching for its dinner. With webbed feet and sharp claws, the cat finally nabs a slippery fish. Ignoring the fish's wriggling, the cat clutches its victim firmly in its teeth.

Felis viverrina. *Weight: 17-31 lbs.*

PALLAS' CAT
& Other Little-Known Cats

The forests of northeast India boast the greatest variety of wild cats in the world. The Namdapha Tiger Reserve alone counts a record nine species: tiger, leopard, clouded leopard, snow leopard, marbled cat, golden cat, leopard cat, jungle cat, and fishing cat. Elsewhere in Asia, the flat-headed cat, bay cat, rusty-spotted cat, and Pallas' cat make their home. Outside of protected reserves such as Namdapha, however, the future of Asian cats is being threatened by the destruction of forests, especially for cultivation, and by hunting, which includes hunting cats for food.

PALLAS' CAT
Felis manul. *Weight: 6.5-11 lbs.*

Far from the cats of the Oriental region lives Pallas' cat, which is found mainly in steppe country from the Caspian to northeastern China, and south to Iran, Afghanistan, Ladakh, and Tibet. Pallas' cat, named after a German naturalist, is about the size of a large domestic cat. Its fur is yellow or ochre tinged silvery-grey, with a trace of black on the head and back. It is characterized by a flat head profile in which the ears are wide apart and spread horizontally. These adaptations seem to help the cat keep a low profile when stalking in open country with little cover.

SAND CAT
Felis margarita. *Weight: 4-5 lbs.*

The arid deserts of the world stand as inhospitable barriers to the spread of animals. Nevertheless, a small cat has found its niche among the sand dunes of the world's fiercest deserts, including the Sahara and the Arabian desert. There the tiny sand cat has evolved a thick coat which insulates it from the alternating intense heat and cold. The pads on its feet are covered with dense hair, which protects them from hot sand and provides a grip on the shifting surface. The cat stretches out on its back to keep cool. During the heat of the day the sand cat rests in a

When stalking, the amber-colored Pallas' cat (above and left) flattens its ears to help it escape detection. The small cat is built sturdily to survive its cold mountain environment.

Conserving its body moisture with a thick coat, the tiny sand cat (above) has found its niche in arid African deserts. It seldom finds water, but manages to get enough moisture from the bodies of prey it has killed.

burrow dug in the shade of bushes or small mounds, emerging in the coolness of dusk to hunt rodents such as gerbils. It sometimes hunts by day when prey are active. The sand cat seldom, if ever, gets a chance to drink, but obtains sufficient moisture from the bodies of its prey.

The sand cat was first found in the Sahara desert during a French expedition led by Gen. Jean-Auguste Margueritte, in whose honor the cat was named.

Seventy years later, Soviet scientists discovered a similar cat in a Turkmenistan desert. It was described as a separate species, largely because it was difficult to believe any connection existed between it and the Algerian specimen, given that they were 3,000 miles apart.

However, the British explorer Wilfred Thesiger brought back a skin from Saudi Arabia, and later, scientists obtained some live specimens. They were intermediate in size between the Algerian and Turkmenistan

cats. Later still the sand cat was found in a Pakistani desert, so that now it is known that the cats are the same species and live through the great belt of deserts from North Africa to Central Asia.

The sand cat has prominent triangular ears, without tufts, and a highly developed auditory system, which helps it to locate prey. Add the cat's remarkable loud barking, and it seems well-equipped to communicate with its kind in the vast dunes. Similar features have evolved in desert foxes.

The sand cat usually gives birth to about four cubs, which spontaneously start to dig in the sand with their forepaws when only five weeks old.

Because it lives in such inhospitable areas, little is known about the status of the sand cat, but in Pakistan it is considered close to possible extinction, largely because commercial hunters have avidly sought it for zoos and collectors. Easily captured, sand cats were grabbed as they basked outside their burrows, which seems to testify to the cats' unfamiliarity with humans.

CHINESE DESERT CAT
Felis bieti. *Average weight: 12 lbs.*

Another so-called "desert cat," this feline actually does not inhabit deserts at all. It frequents rocky steppes and forest- or bush-covered mountains in the western Chinese provinces of Gansu and Sichuan near the border with Tibet.

Larger than a domestic cat, the Chinese desert cat has a yellowish-grey coat. Its cheeks have two brownish streaks, and there are also streaks on its haunches. Its ears are tipped with long black hairs, nearly an inch in length. Its tail has three or four black rings and ends with a blackish tip.

Virtually nothing is known of the life of this small cat. A single anecdote repeated in the literature tells of a hunter's adventure-some dog being bitten twice on the jaw when it chased a desert cat.

MARBLED CAT
Felis marmorata. *Average weight: 12 lbs.*

The marbled cat looks somewhat like a small clouded leopard, even having webbed toes and double claw sheaths like the clouded leopard's. It is the size of a domestic cat, with blackish stripes on the head, neck, and back and large blotches which merge to give the marbled effect. The marbled cat appears to be nocturnal and arboreal. An early observer once watched it stalking a bird along the branch of a tree. He shot it before it completed its maneuver, but he produced a drawing to illustrate its stalk.

Black blotches and stripes combine to give the marbled cat (above) its name. A rare cat that dwells in the forest, it is one of several small felines seldom studied by scientists.

Unlike some other Asian species, the widespread leopard cat (left) is holding its own in range and numbers. The rare Iriomote cat (below) is not so fortunate, however; *only a few dozen of its kind remain on one rugged Japanese island. The elongated muzzle and strong jaw muscles of the flat-headed cat (bottom) help it seize fish, a favorite prey.*

LEOPARD CAT

Felis bengalensis. *Weight: 6.5-15 lbs.*

Least threatened as a species is the beautiful leopard cat, which is found from the extreme west of the Indian subcontinent through China, Korea, and the Soviet Far East and on the islands of Taiwan, Philippines, Borneo, Java, Bali, and Sumatra. The leopard cat is about the size of a domestic cat and, as the name suggests, is spotted like a leopard. The Chinese once called it the "money cat" because the spots resembled Chinese money.

The leopard cat is found in forested habitat, seems to be catholic in its prey, and sometimes has been known to live near human settlements.

IRIOMOTE CAT

Felis iriomotensis. *Weight: not available*

Remote from other cats, a small brown spotted cat evolved on the little island of Iriomote, about 100 miles east of Taiwan. It was only discovered by scientists in the 1960s, although local people had always known it.

Pronounced a new genus, *Mayailurus*, it was thought to link Asian cats with the jaguarundi of tropical America. However, scientists now generally agree that it is another species of *felis*, most closely related to the leopard cat.

Deforestation and overhunting of its principal prey (dwarf wild pig) have already reduced the Iriomote cat, so that it is seriously threatened with extinction. Only about 40 to 80 cats remain.

FLAT-HEADED CAT

Felis planiceps. *Weight: 12-17.5 lbs.*

The flat-headed cat of peninsular Malaysia, Borneo, and Sumatra prefers to hunt fish and a variety of small mammals and birds, but will also attack chickens.

It shares the fishing cat's resemblance to civets and cannot fully retract its claws, but it also sports features of the weasel family. The

long sloping forehead and muzzle shape are very noticeable. It is about the size of a domestic cat, dark brown, and without stripes or spots except for white facial markings on the inside of the eyes and on the muzzle and chin.

ASIAN GOLDEN CAT
Felis temmincki. *Weight: 13-26 lbs.*

The Asian golden cat, or Temminck's cat, is especially interesting because it appears to be closely related to the African golden cat (*F. aurata*), although the two species are separated by more than 4,000 miles. It is thought that about one million years ago forests covered the area from Senegal to China, a region now broken by vast deserts. Over the years, the deserts probably isolated the two golden cat populations.

Temminck's cat, named in honor of the Dutch zoologist who described the African species, has fur of various shades of gold to dark brown, even black, some with spots like a leopard cat and others almost plain. A few black and white stripes cross the cheeks and run down the forehead.

The golden cat roams the forests from Nepal and northeast India through southeast Asia, southern China, Sumatra, and Borneo.

Separated by 4,000 miles, the Asian golden cat (below) still shares many features with the African golden cat. The two were probably once one species, which over time was divided into two species by vast stretches of desert.

It usually preys on small deer, hares, birds, and reptiles, but it has also killed sheep, goats, and water buffalo calves.

In Burma and Thailand, the golden cat is called "fire tiger." The Karen people believe that carrying a single hair from the cat keeps tigers away, while others believe that burning the hair deters tigers.

BAY CAT
Felis badia. *Weight: 4-6.5 lbs.*

On the island of Borneo lives a smaller relative of the golden cat, the bay cat, which has a chestnut coat with indistinct spots underneath and on the limbs. It is probably the least known of the Asian cats and has seldom been seen by naturalists. In Sarawak, zoologist Tom Harrison obtained and observed one bay cat specimen, which preferred areas of rocky limestone on the edge of the jungle. Harrison suspected it ate offal as well as small live prey.

RUSTY-SPOTTED CAT
Felis rubiginosus. *Weight: 2-4.5 lbs.*

The rusty-spotted cat is a rare cat of Sri Lanka and southern India. In 1975, however, the Zoological Society of India collected a specimen far to the north in Kashmir.

Strangely, the cat inhabits the humid forests in Sri Lanka, but not the arid northern part of the island, while in southern India it frequents arid areas.

The nineteenth-century British naturalist T. C. Jerdon said he had as a pet a very tame rusty-spotted kitten, which hunted squirrels in the rafters. When introduced to a young gazelle, the kitten grabbed it immediately by the nape and had to be pulled off.

The rusty-spotted cat is smaller than a domestic cat, has cheek stripes, and is generally grey-brown with rust-brown spots on the back and flanks. So far as is known, it is primarily nocturnal, hunting small mammals, reptiles, and birds. Some Sri Lankan villagers are reported to catch and eat it.

Found only in Sri Lanka and southern India, the rusty-spotted cat (left) is one of the world's rarest species. Usually prowling by night, the little cat catches rodents, birds, and small mammals.

FOREST WILDCAT

The fierce forest wildcat sometimes breeds with domestic cats, which often makes it difficult to identify a true wildcat.

Felis sylvestris. *Weight: 6.5-13 lbs.*

"The British tiger—the fiercest and most destructive beast we have, making dreadful havoc among our poultry, lambs and kids." So wrote Thomas Pennant, an eighteenth-century naturalist, of the wild cat *Felis sylvestris.* Throughout Britain it was mercilessly treated as vermin, so that by the mid-nineteenth century, it was nearly extinct except in the wilds of Scotland, where it still survives today.

The wildcat got the same treatment elsewhere in Europe. Humans extinguished it from vast areas, and it survives only in the forests of central, southern, and eastern parts of the continent. The wildcat remains hostile to humans to this day, throwing itself on its back and raking frantically with its claws when approached.

Often larger than the domestic cat, the forest wildcat has dense, long fur, greyish with stripes of black, and a ringed, black-tipped tail. It was once considered to be one of many species of cats in Africa and Eurasia, including the African wildcat and Asian wildcat. Now, most researchers consider wildcats to be one group with several races widely distributed over Europe, Asia, and Africa. The wildcat's domesticated descendants are our pets.

Although the road from captivity to tranquil domestic life must have been a long one, Egyptians found they could domesticate the African wildcat. After coming to Europe as pets in Greece and Rome, wildcats spread, mating with forest wildcats. Crossbreeding occurs today between domestic cats and wildcats, making it difficult to distinguish a true wildcat. The "pollution" of the wildcat's genes is considered a threat, yet throughout Europe and as far east as the Caucasus, the forest wildcat has made a comeback.

Forest wildcats hunt by day or by night, depending on local conditions and availability of prey. They are usually solitary, but sometimes they hunt in pairs or as a family group, possibly giving them an advantage when prey flushed out by one cat is grabbed by the waiting partner. Normal fare includes small mammals, reptiles, and birds. Rodent remains were found in 99 percent of feces collected during recent studies in France; rabbit, hare, and bird remains were found in only three percent of the collected feces. The cats also eat fish and even grasshoppers.

The mating ritual is similar to that of the domestic cat, with males competing for a female, and both sexes announcing their desires by loud caterwauling. The female establishes her lair among rocks, in old fox dens, under stumps, and sometimes in birds' nests. After a gestation of about 60 days, two to four cubs are born. After 10 to 12 weeks they are already going hunting with their mother, and at three months are independent. As cubs, they are threatened by snakes and other predators, but once grown, they can often escape enemies.

LYNX

The Spanish lynx, slightly smaller than the north European lynx and more uniformly spotted, once ranged throughout the Iberian peninsula. Today, however, it survives only in scattered small populations in central and southern Spain and Portugal.

The Spanish lynx depends heavily on rabbits, whose drastic decline in numbers has been a major factor in the parallel decline of the lynx. Myxomatosis (a virus) has wiped out many rabbits. Goat herding once maintained good rabbit habitat, but it has given way to agriculture. Deforestation, too, has trimmed the lynx population.

One of the lynx's strongholds has been the Doñana National Park near Seville, Spain. Once a remote hunting preserve, it is now surrounded by beach resorts, eucalyptus plantations, and rice fields. Only 25 years ago, an expedition led by British naturalist Guy Mountfort reported 150 to 200 lynxes in the park. Now, according to Miguel Delibes, the specialist on Doñana's lynxes, only 30 to 40 remain. Hunters kill some lynxes illegally, and many lynxes die in snares set for rabbits. With new roadbuilding, especially a fast road to the coast, cars now run over some lynxes. In the Toledo mountains, conservationists are protesting a plan to convert lynx habitat into an air force bombing range.

The Spanish lynx (*Lynx lynx pardina*) is a sub-species of the northern European lynx (*Lynx lynx*), regarded by many as the same animal which roams Canada and the northern United States (See page 52).

Although lynxes are somewhat abundant in Soviet forests and eastern Asia, the pressure on the lynx has been great in Europe, where forests have been cut down. Efforts have been made, however, to return lynxes to their native habitat. A group was reintroduced in Yugoslavia in 1973.

In 1975, nine lynxes were released in central Austria. Scientists hoped these cats might someday link up with the Yugoslavian population. The well-funded effort was supported heartily by game management chiefs in several cities. Most hunters opposed the idea, however, fearing the lynx would be too effective a competitor for deer.

The transplanted lynxes were monitored closely. Deer kills did begin to show up, with lynxes killing more red deer than expected in one area. The high numbers of humans nearby also caused the lynxes to roam farther than scientists had predicted. As a result, local landowners, farmers, and hunters expressed concerns which were never satisfactorily answered. The project, which went well from a scientific point of view, thus ran into severe public relations problems.

Most scientists believe the European lynx (below) is related to the lynx found in snowy northern regions of North America. Yet the Spanish lynx (left) is usually considered a rare sub-species of the European lynx.

Lynx pardina. *Average weight: 26 lbs.*

AFRICA

BY NORMAN MYERS

LION

Lions are not animals alone. They are symbols and totems and legends. They have impressed themselves so deeply on the human mind, if not its blood, it is as though the psyche were emblazoned with their crest.

—Evelyn Ames, *A Glimpse of Eden*

According to fable, a lion once went hunting with a fox, a jackal, and a wolf. The quartet killed a stag, and while the others argued how the carcass was to be divided, the lion ordered it to be cut into four parts. He claimed the first one because he was king of the beasts, the second one because he was arbiter of the case, and the third one because of his part in the hunt. As for the last one, he would take it as well—unless the others cared to challenge him. Thus was born the phrase, "the lion's share."

The fable, it seems, is not too far from the truth. Male lions typically leave the killing to the females, then insist on feeding first on the carcass. No matter whether male or female lions are eating, other individual animals, even hyenas, seem to keep their distance until the powerful cats have had first crack at the meat.

The "lion's share" is no idle phrase, but a good description of how lions get something they want—directly and with force. Likewise, the story is one of many recounted to explain how the lion, perceived as the mightiest of the world's cats, relates to the rest of the world.

The lion has long enjoyed a preeminent reputation in the symbolism, folklore, and religion of cultures throughout the world. The Assyrians and Babylonians named constellations after the lion. In Africa, it symbolized power. Some tribal chiefs, for instance, used staffs such as the one at right, which illustrates the adage, "Only the lion drinks from the palm-wine pot of the leopard." Loosely interpreted, that means some chiefs are more powerful than others. In Greek mythology the lion served as a symbol of watchfulness, often associated with the sun; in Egypt it was revered in the form of the Sphinx, a lion with a human face.

Yet the lion sometimes suffered a darker portrayal: in the biblical story of Daniel, the seven lions symbolized the seven deadly sins. In the New Testament, Peter enjoins his readers to be on guard against the devil, who "as a roaring lion, walketh about seeking whom he may devour."

In England, the lion found a prominent spot in heraldry, where it was portrayed as royal by nature, proud and generous. King Richard I of England was known as the Lion-Hearted; Scotland put an upright, scarlet lion on its yellow flag.

Humans have labeled the lion "King of the Beasts," but no such thing really exists. Like other predators, the lion simply kills to survive. Being large and strong—a male can weigh as much as 530 pounds and stretch nine feet long—it does an unusually good job of defending itself when necessary; but it is not particularly brave or magnanimous.

The air of strength is underlined by the

In some African tribes, staffs with a carved lion figure signified the chief's power.

Hunting big cats was once a sport reserved for kings such as the Assyrian Ashurnasirpal, who shot lions with arrows from his chariot (below). Those lions often were not wild, but had been bred in captivity and then released just for the hunt. An ancient gold coin (right) from the Mughal empire in India combines two powerful symbols, a lion and a rising sun.

In Greek mythology, King Eurystheus gave Hercules twelve tasks to test his strength, the hardest of which was slaying the Nemean lion, seen on the vase above. After his club and arrows failed, Hercules strangled the lion and returned home with it in triumph.

lion's spectacular roaring—mighty sounds that vibrate like thunder to advertise the lion's presence. Necessary to delineate a pride's home range and to communicate with other cats, roaring is so important that lions in the middle of a meal have stopped eating to let loose with the awesome sound.

While both males and females roar, only the male boasts the large golden and/or black ruff around its face. The mane seems to intimidate rivals, and possibly lionesses. It also protects the neck during fights.

Even though its appearance gives regal vibrations, the lion is far from the creature of popular renown. Rather than being a proud predator, for example, the lion is often a downright scavenger. As biologists George Schaller and Hans Kruuk revealed, a substantial amount of the lion's food is robbed from other killers—often from hyenas. Lions on the treeless Serengeti scavenged for 53 percent of their food, one study showed.

If the lion's hunting methods do not reflect much dignity on the animal, neither do the lion's social systems reflect what humans traditionally believed about the cat. The idea once prevailed that lordly males established the pride's home range and defended it against trespassers. To some extent this is true. But in fact, much of the work of establishing the pride and its range and maintaining stability is left up to the lionesses.

ANDROCLES AND THE LION

Nothing scientists have observed suggests that a lion is particularly gentle or noble, yet tales extolling the lion's kindness extend back to the ancient story of "Androcles and the Lion."

Androcles, a Roman slave, runs away from his cruel master. In search of food in the forest, Androcles comes upon a moaning lion. To his astonishment, the lion does not spring on him, but holds out a swollen and bleeding paw. Androcles pulls out a huge thorn and bandages the paw. The grateful lion takes the runaway slave to his cave and brings him meat every day.

One day both Androcles and the lion are captured, and the slave is sentenced to be thrown to the lions in a public spectacle. When Androcles is cast out into the arena, however, he is met by the lion he befriended earlier. The lion turns and fights to save his friend from certain death. The crowd is so amazed that both Androcles and the lion are given their freedom.

This tale has been told in various forms, including one version featuring St. Jerome (right), who was reported to have removed a thorn from a lion's paw. The tale also supplied George Bernard Shaw with the crux of his play *Androcles and the Lion.*

Except for fights over food, life in a pride is usually relatively harmonious, and lions stand a better chance of survival living communally in a pride than living alone. A pride can contain three to forty lions—generally several related lionesses with their young and one to four adult males.

At its heart, a lion pride is a closed sisterhood of female adults, usually related to each other. Though the boundaries of a pride's home range may shift slightly due to abundance of prey or outside pressures, in general, a pride passes on the same territory from one generation to another.

Lionesses reveal an exceptional capacity for cooperation. They hunt together with some degree of coordinated tactics, which enables them to be much more successful than if operating as individuals. Lion cubs are brought up in something approaching communal style. While a lioness gives preference to her own cubs when they want to nurse, she will allow those of other pride members to join in too.

In contrast to this cooperation, the males of the pride contribute to the pride's stability by keeping out transient males.

A pride's home range varies from 20 square miles to 100, depending on the abundance of game. Hearing the lions roaring in the inky shadows of night warns possible trespassers that the pride has staked out the neighborhood as its own.

Maintaining its own piece of savanna is basic to the existence of the pride. Females drive away strange females from the home range, and males do battle with male intruders, but females have been known to drive off nomadic males, as well. Since nomadic males covet the pride and its territory, fights between males are often savage, sometimes to the point of death. Schaller estimated that 5.5 percent of the fights ended in death to a combatant.

Although females appear to perform some of the territorial defense, the males are most likely the final arbiters. When a ranking male was killed in the Serengeti National Park in Tanzania, reported Schaller, the pride's territory declined and the survival rate of cubs dropped drastically, possibly because the shift in home range boundaries resulted in less prey being available.

In a variant to these social dynamics in the Serengeti, lions in Nairobi Park seem to undergo a major change in numbers and range occupancy about every two years. Biologist Judith Rudnai, who watched these lions over several years in the 1970s, found that prides and home ranges remained relatively stable for a period, then a major exodus of lions occurred toward areas outside the park. Months later, many of these straying lions reappeared, but by that time the resident prides had broken up. So new associations were formed, such as sister with sister and mother with daughter.

This biennial readjustment of the social system seems to coincide with the length of time it takes for one generation to attain maturity and become independent. The pattern ties in with the findings of Pierre DesMeules at Ngorongoro Crater and of Schaller in the Serengeti, who discovered that the breeding cycles of lionesses within a pride somehow become synchronized, causing several litters of cubs to be brought up together within a few months of each other.

The cubs are kept secluded from the pride for the first six weeks. After making their debut as members of the pride, however, the youngsters become bundles of energetic curiosity, and the mother lion must be ever watchful to keep them in line. The pride helps to protect the little ones, as well, especially from predation.

Before it can be an effective hunter, a newborn lion has much growing to do. Cubs are weaned at six or seven months, and their permanent teeth erupt between the ninth and twelfth months, causing some pain. By the time the cubs have cut their teeth, however, the rains usually have come, and the grass is lush. Soon, the plains are full of prey.

Herds of wildebeest, Thomson's gazelles, and zebras travel the African plains, and life is bounteous for the lions. When the rains

A lioness can be a good provider, but in lean times her needs come first, and the survival rate of cubs drops. Starvation, predation, and abandonment kill two-thirds of the cubs, according to zoologist George Schaller.

Secure in this scene, a cub depends on its mother for almost two years. Then young males must search for their own pride and home range. Females usually remain with the pride in which they were born.

cease, however, the herds of prey migrate over the rolling hillsides to more wooded areas where water and foliage remain. Then life for the lions becomes more difficult. Driven by hunger on the dry and dusty plains, they sometimes attack larger animals such as elephants—but the result is more often broken teeth than a satisfying meal.

Whatever the season, the pride hunts in more or less the same fashion. Able to see across open plains in every direction, lions can easily pinpoint prey by sight, and then keep visual contact with each other to carry out a coordinated hunting strategy. During the usual stalk, a pride sometimes fans out in a sort of V-shape, like a human army executing a pincer movement on an enemy's flank. Some of the group then charges, herding the victim into the waiting jaws of the other lions. Once a kill has been made, the cats try to move it to a quiet place to eat.

Opportunistic creature that it is, the lion does not spurn small fry for its meals. Although it is the only hunter big enough to tackle buffalo, giraffe, and young elephants, the lion also eats antelopes, birds, fish, reptiles, and whatever carrion it comes across. According to scientist Fritz Eloff, lions in the Kalahari Desert of southern Africa eat hares and similar small mammals to sustain themselves during lean periods.

Since a lion can weigh several hundred pounds, it needs a large and steady supply of calories to survive, but it tends to eat in periodic gorgings rather than every day. In a single session, a male lion can consume as much as 80 pounds of meat, or one-quarter of his body weight. That's equivalent to a man plowing his way through a 40-pound steak. After such a meal, a lion does not need to eat for a whole week.

Scientists have debated how many animals are needed to satisfy the lion's appetite, estimating from 10 to 35 medium-sized animals (such as wildebeest and zebra) per lion per year. However, lions do not eat the

Lionesses will let any cub in the pride nurse (below) and they seem to enjoy playful games with the youngsters (right). Rambunctious cubs practice skills by wrestling in mock combat (far right) and stalking moving objects, even fellow cubs.

entire animal, often leaving hooves, horns, or other parts behind. So it may be more accurate to talk about how many pounds of meat a lion actually needs to survive. Scientist George Schaller believes that a lion may need 5,600 pounds of meat a year and a lioness around 4,000 pounds.

A number of the animals that lions eat are sick, lame, old, or young. In the Serengeti, for instance, the prey population increased fourfold between 1960 and 1980, primarily because of better rainfall. Clearly the lions and other carnivores had little effect on the population explosion in that instance.

New findings, new theories, constant changes. We now know far more about lions than we did twenty years ago, and we know more about lions than about almost any other wild cat. Despite all that scientists have found out, it is plain that we have hardly begun to understand lion ecology.

The revelations of Schaller's study in the Serengeti differ significantly, for instance, from those of a researcher investigating lions in Kivu Park in eastern Zaire, where lions prey principally on hippos. In Lake Manyara Park, adjacent to Ngorongoro in Kenya, buffalos in thick woods wind up being the prey 62 percent of the time—and that difference affects the lions' hunting tactics and their own mortality. In South Africa's Kruger National Park, on the other hand, gnus top the list of prey, which affects the hunting strategies of lions there.

Lions also prey on waterbuck in Kruger Park, but waterbuck are largely disregarded in Rwenzori Park in western Uganda, several hundred miles to the north. While it may

Zebras shimmer in the midday heat (above) as young adult lions watch, just observing for now. Lions seem to hunt primarily by sight, and have little stamina for a long chase. Their favorite hunting time is at dusk or dawn, but if prey can be found at night, then the pride willingly goes after it.

seem self-evident, it is wise to remember that the lion's behavior and response to a given environment varies from place to place, season to season.

Fortunately, lions can live in every part of wildland Africa except the very dry and the very wet zones. Except for the few remaining lions in Asia, lions are creatures of the tropics, favoring grasslands or wooded savannas. There, the lions' tawny coats aid in concealment, since the grass is brown most of the time. The lion seems especially at home in southern Kenya and northern Tanzania, probably because of the vast herds of zebras, wildebeest, gazelles, and other prey.

Regrettably, the savannas are precisely the same places best suited for expanding human communities. Peasants pursuing agricultural lifestyles, naturally enough, prefer lightly wooded grasslands to thick

bush areas, since farming and raising livestock are easier in open plains.

Of course, it may be all too easy for an urban American to call for preservation of the open plains and the lions that live on them. To understand the problems of wildlife conservation, an honest observer must also assess the situation from the point of view of the people directly affected by the wild animals: the farmer who needs crops to feed his family more than he needs the migrating game herds that may live on that same land.

So great are the land needs of farmers that in eastern Kenya, some communities are reputed to be expanding at double-digit annual percentages. Similar pressures are emerging in Tanzania, Zambia, and Cameroon. Moreover, a plant geneticist in Kenya has developed a strain of corn that will grow in as little as ten inches of rain per season,

which means that even wider tracts of wild-land Africa are now open to settlement by farmers. This discovery is tougher news for the lion's future than the activities of thousands of poachers.

So what is a lion, a truly wild lion living in its natural African environment? That is something we may never know, since most lions no longer roam freely across untrammeled stretches of wilderness Africa.

In light of evidence from the main countries of its range, the lion has been undergoing decline in both habitat and numbers. The lion could well be down to fewer than 50,000 by now, or about one fourth as many as 50 years ago.

Generally speaking, the reason for this decline is loss of living space as growing numbers of humans take over plains and savannas where wildlife used to roam. In the

lion's case, special problems arise because some stock raisers squeeze wild herbivores off their land, depriving lions of their usual prey. The lions then begin to maraud domestic herds. In contrast, when the usual prey of the leopard disappears, the cat can subsist off much smaller natural prey, such as birds and rodents.

Because lions do not hesitate to scavenge, they are vulnerable to poisoned pieces of meat left lying around. Some ranchers and farmers leave poisoned bait to kill animals they perceive as a threat to their own crops or herds. Furthermore, the lion is easily tracked down by a disenchanted rancher with a gun.

But conservation, like politics, is not for ivory-tower idealists, and one must make the best of the situation. If lions were eventually confined to parks and reserves in Africa, many of them might not fare too badly.

The advantage of hunting in groups is evident when lions tackle prey such as this giraffe (above). But after the prey is subdued, it's usually "every one for himself," as lions fiercely shoulder their way in to feed (above right). They bite, snarl, and snap at each other while feeding, but then may lick each other's wounds. Like most cats, they like to drink after eating a meal.

Savanna Africa's protected areas now total almost 200,000 square miles, an area larger than California. Some of these immense stretches of country contain good numbers of lions. For instance, Kruger Park, in South Africa, numbers 1,200 lions, and Serengeti's ecosystem features more than 2,000 lions.

In some places, the lion's existence furthers the cause of wildlife conservation overall. In Amboseli Park, Kenya, for instance, several dozen lions help to generate tourist revenues in the form of park fees and stopover payments at the local game lodge. According to Wes Henry and David Western, an Amboseli lion with suitably shaggy mane is worth $515,000 per year (late 1970s value) by virtue of its attractiveness to tourists. Were it to be made available to a sportsman hunter, it would be worth a mere $8,500 for (so to speak) a one-shot occasion. This heartening note of the lion's value as a tourist attraction, however, will not ensure the lion's future.

Lions once ranged from Greece to central India, but by 100 A.D. they were gone from Europe. Extinction in nineteenth century India was linked to human hunting; today, loss of habitat is a more serious threat. Overgrazing by livestock is rapidly turning forest into desert. In Asia, the lion has been reduced to about 200 individuals in the Gir Forest preserve.

In Africa, populations that were thriving as recently as the mid-1960s are now mere remnants of their more robust past. Of course the lion is still hanging on in these areas, and occasional individuals can still be seen. But that raises a question: What consti-

A powerful hunger for some remaining scraps of zebra (on ground, left) brings a lioness and a black-maned male into battle. Lions live a life of indolence (right), interrupted now and then by brief dramas of hunting or fighting. Depending on their success in hunting, they may spend as much as 18 to 20 hours a day resting.

For lions, mating is a fierce and frequent affair. At first, the female may growl or act coy (below). Copulation (top right) lasts about 20 seconds, during which the male may bite the female's neck. He dismounts quickly, though (bottom right), since the female is likely to turn abruptly and slap or bite him. A pair may copulate several times over a 24-hour period.

tutes "adequate conservation status" for a large predator that maintains only moderate numbers even in favorable habitats?

To respond to this question, we should take account of a factor that is central to the survival of a species: gene pools, and their critical minimum size. To avoid the human equivalent of cousins marrying cousins, lions must be able to breed easily with partners who have a markedly different set of genes.

In the case of the lion, many populations are becoming isolated, with no further gene exchange possible with other populations. This applies notably to lions in protected parks and reserves, such as Amboseli in Kenya, Lake Manyara in Tanzania, and Kabalega in Uganda. This regrettable situation will soon overtake still more lion populations. What is the point, one might ask, in safeguarding a lion population in parks and reserves if, in another century or so, the survivors start to "grow two heads"?

We have scant knowledge of the genetics of wild lion populations—how much gene variability they have, how much is necessary to maintain a viable genetic pool, and how feasible artificial gene exchange might someday be. Some scientists at zoos have found variability can be maintained with a certain number of animals. But how much space they need, and in what kind of ecology, is a different matter. Thus a greater percentage of money and scientific skills might be spent on gene research than is now the case.

Conservation should concern itself with the needs of the future, as well as with the demands of the present. With half a billion people, Africa is already overcrowded, and every day, the region takes on board many more newcomers, all in need of food and a place to make a living. If we are to help the lion survive in its wild haunts, we should increase our efforts now. Otherwise the African lion could eventually follow the dismal track of the lion in Asia—a few dozen holdouts, roaming a preserve.

Lions top the list of tourist attractions in Africa's wildlands. A lion in Amboseli Park with an average life span of 15 years could attract almost $7.75 million in tourist dollars, making it one of the most valuable animals on earth.

LEOPARD

The leopard, hunter without equal, is a loner. No other animal appears so much to be its own creature, like poet Rudyard Kipling's cat that "walks by himself . . . all on his wild lone."

Panthera pardus.
Weight: males, 82-200 lbs. females, 61-133 lbs.

A beautiful combination of grace and power, the leopard is compact muscle and flowing movement, all in one body. One of the most accomplished feline stalkers, the leopard slinks from one patch of scrub to another, inconspicuous, infinitely patient, in search of food. The leopard can creep very close to its prey, revealing itself for only a few seconds at the instant of attack. Adult leopards measure about two feet high and seven feet long. How such a creature sneaks unseen and unheard across an area covered only by sparse vegetation is a mystery. But the stealthiest of the great cats often succeeds at it, emerging in a rush to snare its prey.

One hot afternoon in the Serengeti National Park, as dusk was closing in, a leopard stalked a herd of gazelles near a stream. As it crept through a hundred yards of grass, the unwary gazelles grazed in a tall tangle of reeds nearer the water. When the leopard reached the thicker growth, it disappeared. Five minutes passed, then half an hour, and still nothing happened.

The leopard's spotted coat matched the clumps of vegetation almost perfectly. It might have been behind that bush, or it might have not, for all the human eye could see. Such camouflage allows the leopard to be equally at home in the forest or in the open grasslands, making it a versatile hunter.

That day by the stream, the leopard's patience and stealth paid off. With no sound to betray it, the leopard suddenly materialized alongside the gazelles, which scattered headlong, sounding a chorus of alarm notes. A moment later, the leopard sat gripping its prize: a kicking, full-grown gazelle.

As soon as the gazelle's thrashing came to a stop, the leopard set off toward a nearby tree with the carcass in tow. It plainly wanted to get its booty out of the reach of other hungry carnivores. Dragging the 50-pound gazelle, the leopard had to pause a couple of times, panting to catch its breath. Yet the leopard did not give up. It simply got a better grip on the carcass and plunged ahead. To appreciate the leopard's power, one has to see it bound up a tree, carrying a weight at least half its own.

This day—still clutching the gazelle in its jaws—the leopard lunged for the tree's lowest branch, about six feet off the ground. Not satisfied the prize was safe, the leopard lugged its kill still higher, until it reached a point at least 25 feet high, out of reach of even the most enterprising scavenger.

Leopards do not bury uneaten meat for a later meal, as many cats do. Leopards readily gulp down meat that has been sitting in the searing African heat for days. Flesh, maggots, and buzzing flies all go down together with no apparent ill effects on the leopard.

For a human, seeing a leopard catching its prey, especially in daylight, is unusual. Such events are most likely witnessed in the protected parks of Africa, where leopards have grown accustomed to human visitors. On occasion, they may bask on a branch in broad sunlight, even when a safari truck loaded with camera-clicking tourists rumbles up.

Outside of the reserves, however, the leopard seems exceptionally cautious and is seldom seen. Cat expert C. A. W. Guggisberg reports the tale of an Indian villager who was asked by an Englishman whether a particular leopard was cunning. Replied the man, "Sahib! Where that leopard walks, he brushes out his tracks with his tail."

Many leopards live within a few miles of communities. Even if local people do not come across its tracks, they still realize that no other hunter could soundlessly snatch a dog from the doorway of a village hut.

The leopard's graceful trademark tail, dangling elegantly from a tree like a velvet rope, may sometimes betray the leopard's lofty perch. More often, a human sees only movement merging into shadow. The leopard's hoarse cough may announce its presence, but seeing the cat itself—well, that's a

different matter. From a hundred yards away, even the most brightly-colored leopard blends effortlessly into the shade.

It is in the hours of darkness, however, that the leopard seems to truly find its element. The cat can lurk in suitable cover, waiting for its prey to come along. Or the leopard can survey the territory where prey has been found before, listening as baboons and monkeys scramble for cover. In the daytime, an adult baboon can see the leopard and may even wrangle with it over rights to a kill. At night, however, the odds rest with the leopard, and the baboon could just as easily become the leopard's next meal.

The leopard negotiates in silence, walking with each forepaw turned inward. The outer edge of the paw strikes the ground first, and objects likely to cause noise can be avoided before the leopard's full weight comes down.

Because of its hunting technique, silent and solitary, the opportunistic leopard is able to live off a much broader spectrum of prey

Early Egyptians created this gold leopard head (above), which was found in the tomb of Tutankhamen ("King Tut"), unearthed in 1922. Greek historian Pliny the Elder described the leopard as having a distinctive sweet breath which attracted and subdued other animals. This drawing from an illuminated medieval English manuscript (right) depicts the legend.

HOW THE LEOPARD GOT ITS SPOTS

In reality, the leopard's spotted coat serves as effective camouflage in the shadows of the forest. But in legend, its spots have often caused the leopard to be regarded as a creature of evil or deceit. The leopard has symbolized sin, death, and the anti-Christ.

Just how the spots came about is a story in itself, with variations from country to country. One Sierra Leone story says the Leopard was friendly with Fire, going to see him every day. Leopard begged Fire to return the visits, and Fire agreed—if Leopard would prepare a path of dry leaves to his door. After complying, Leopard and his wife heard a commotion at the door, and found Fire there. Leopard leapt away from Fire's flame. But ever since, leopards have been marked with black spots or scorch marks from the fingers of Fire.

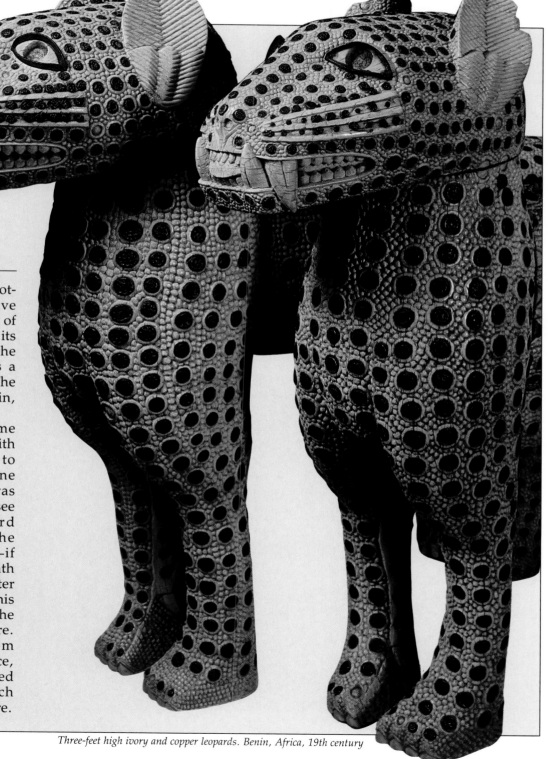

Three-feet high ivory and copper leopards. Benin, Africa, 19th century

In pursuit of a baboon (top), the agile leopard moves into high gear across the sand. For some unknown reason, this doomed baboon whirled to face its death. Within seconds it was killed with a bite to the neck. A bush pig (below) tries to escape the same fate.

than the lion or cheetah can. When the opportunity presents itself, the leopard hunts animals of the 150-pound class, such as impalas and young zebras. It also kills smaller creatures such as dik-diks and klip-springers. At times it eats birds, rats, frogs, fish, and snakes.

The leopard's strong hunting instinct and intuition show up in cubs at an early age. Leopard cubs quickly learn what prey is within their ability to capture, and how best to approach it. Imitation of their mother pays off. Before a cub is a year old, it may make a passable stalk and kill an animal on its own.

Being a good hunter has helped the leopard to survive in many habitats: in every type of forest, in woodlands and savannas, in mountain uplands. Leopards range from Africa to China, from India through the USSR. There is a Leopard Point on the crater rim of Kilimanjaro in Tanzania, and a Leopard Point north of Mombasa, Kenya.

Likewise, the leopard has adapted to the presence of larger cats around it. If leopards coexist in an area with lions or tigers, the leopards appear to allow the larger cats first choice of food and space. Such adaptability in habitat, prey, and living arrangements has served the leopard well. Today, the resilient leopard hangs on in areas where lions and tigers were wiped out long ago.

Some common perceptions of the leopard's behavior are based only on superstition or misinformation. The leopard's supposed inclination to hunt human beings is an example. A colonial game warden in Nigeria, for instance, stated that during the late 1940s a leopard apparently killed dozens of people, most of them women and young children, until it was dispatched by his rifle.

Overleaf: The hunting success of the leopard reflects its strategy and strength: it kills its prey by surprise, stealthily creeping close before striking, then drags the heavy prey to a secure place to eat it.

The habit of storing dead prey in trees is customary among African leopards. A leopard can wedge a springbok carcass, weighing as much as 70 pounds, into the fork of a tree, or drape a dik-dik, its hooves dangling, over a branch. With tomorrow's meal at hand, the cat rests from its labors, while the larder stays safe from scavengers.

After bearing her cubs, the solicitous leopard mother spends months training her brood. Young leopards finally break with the mother at about 22 months, when they depart for a life of hunting.

But there was more to the story. A closer inspection of the leopard revealed that it had lost part of a paw, possibly in a trap. Unable to cope with its normal wild prey, it turned to easier food sources. It became a man-killer not out of choice, but out of necessity. A similar explanation applies to most instances of leopards attacking humans.

The leopard's somewhat sinister reputation has been accentuated by the fact that some leopards are melanistic. Melanism produces a black fur, in which the leopard's usual light background coloring looks as if it has been "dyed" black, leaving the even darker spots to show through only in a certain light. Thus the name "black panther."

Some people believe that black panthers are more powerful and savage than ordinary leopards, but in fact no extra strength comes with the dark color. The color variation is simply the result of a recessive gene. Black leopards can be found in the same litter as ones whose spots show, and they are no more ferocious than their siblings.

In some localities of Africa, man has hunted gazelles, zebras, and wildebeest off the map. In still more places, he has taken over wildlife habitats for his cattle, sheep, and goats, and for his farms and banana plantations. Where this has happened, the lions, cheetahs, and hyenas have quickly faded from the scene. Of the major carnivores, only the adaptable leopard has been able to hang on.

In at least a dozen African countries, the leopard maintains "satisfactory" numbers.

Much of a leopard's time is spent in trees, and some youngsters may fall out while learning to climb. Practice will pay off, however, in superlative climbing skills.

The leopard still seems relatively numerous in forested areas in Zaire and Gabon, although no census has been taken. It also maintains moderate numbers in Tanzania, southern Sudan, Zambia, Cameroon, Botswana, and Mozambique. Of course the leopard's numbers are often low compared with what they *could* be if comprehensive safeguards were in place against illegal hunting of the animal for its skin and widespread poisoning of the animal to protect livestock.

In other countries, notably Kenya and the Central African Republic, the leopard is still years away from "disaster status," though its numbers are a fraction of those in 1960.

Still, the leopard should be considered an imperiled species. Leopard populations are easily poisoned by stock raisers who see their livelihood threatened by wild predators. Though lions, cheetahs, hyenas and other carnivores may kill more sheep and cattle than leopards do, the leopard is more inclined to scavenge than the others (except the hyena). That trait makes it especially susceptible to "treated" meat (poisoned bait deliberately left to kill animals which farmers and ranchers perceive as threats).

Poison can clear whole landscapes of the animal. Major stock-raising countries of Africa (Kenya, Ethiopia, Namibia, and Zimbabwe) have seen nine out of ten of their leopards disappear during the course of the 1970s, many of them victims of poison. The experience of South Africa demonstrates that a country can eliminate virtually all its leopards in relatively short order, leaving only relict populations in parks and reserves.

Nevertheless, the leopard's prospects for survival will probably continue to be better than those of the lion or cheetah. Although its numbers will dwindle as human populations take over more of its natural habitat, the leopard can probably hang on in ravines, desert wadis, moorlands, rain forests, and other types of terrain that are too arid or inaccessible to be easily used by humans.

CHEETAH

Lithe cheetahs are among the most handsome of cats. Strikingly marked, the cheetah's unusual face has a black stripe (the tear stripe) running from the inner corner of each eye. Patterns on the king cheetah (right) may differ from those of the common cheetah, but it is still the same species.

Acinonyx jubatus.
Weight: 110-130 pounds.

On a warm summer's day in eastern Africa, a mother cheetah walked across the savanna with her four cubs. The cubs' smoke-gray fur indicated they were about six weeks old. A few days earlier they would not have been strong enough to accompany her, and, as she had done many times, she would have left them concealed in a clump of withered grass. Leaving them behind always carried a certain amount of risk, however. A cheetah litter generally starts at five or six cubs at birth. But while the mother hunts, the family could well lose some of its members to marauding lions or hyenas.

This day, the cheetah was plainly out on a hunt, with cubs in tow. A cheetah with cubs must kill almost every day if she is to feed not only herself but her offspring.

She stopped periodically to stare at herds of Thomson's gazelles and eventually settled on a group of gazelles about 200 yards away, grazing unconcernedly. Somehow she indicated to her cubs that this was the time for business, and they disappeared beneath a six-inch high scrub patch.

Cautiously, the mother made her way toward the prey, freezing whenever she suspected she was being observed. Soon her low-slung walk accelerated to a trot, then into an all-out burst. A little cloud of dust sped across the grass-sparse plain, in pursuit of the gazelles stampeding in terror.

One gazelle paused a fraction too long, and after less than 200 yards of chase, the lithe, long-legged cheetah pinned it to the ground in a stranglehold. The cheetah's teeth closed around the windpipe until the gazelle died.

The cheetah lay for a while by the carcass, panting. When she recovered her breath, she trotted to the place where she had left the cubs, called them out of hiding, and returned quickly to the carcass.

But it was already too late. A vulture patrolling overhead had spotted the family. The bird alighted nearby. It was soon joined by a second, which had seen the first vulture plunge earthward. Ten vultures gathered and attracted the attention of a jackal. The jackal's expectant gait had, in turn, signaled the interesting news to a spotted hyena lying outside its den half a mile away.

When the cheetah reached the carcass, she disputed ownership of the kill with the vultures. Unless a stronger carnivore opened up the carcass, the vultures could not feed, but meanwhile they stood close guard. Having driven them two dozen yards back, the cheetah began to rip and tear at the prey's abdomen. Every few seconds, she paused to look around with apprehension. Perhaps she sensed that if other predators came to enjoy

*Camouflaged in tall
grass, young cheetahs
await their mother's
return. The mother may
go hunting for up to 36
hours, unavoidably
leaving the young vul-
nerable to predators.*

the meal, the menu might not be limited to the gazelle. Within a few minutes, however, she was feeding in earnest, and the cubs were nibbling the tidbits.

Every few minutes the vultures made a concerted rush, and the mother cheetah started to spend more time fighting them off than feeding. The cubs had to stay close by her to avoid lethal pecks from the vultures' hefty bills.

Suddenly the mother cheetah leaped aside from the carcass. The hyena was approaching at a rush, and across the plain came others of the hyena clan. Hungry as she still was, the cheetah mother did not stand and fight. She might have gotten a nip in the haunches that could make the flat-out chase on the next hunt a painful affair—and anything less than a 60 to 70 mph speed could mean no kill when pursuing a gazelle.

The cubs scattered in a star pattern. This tactic probably serves them well against a single predator, but not so well against pack predators. Even if the cubs were fortunate enough to survive this scene, they would have trouble finding their mother afterward.

The cubs do have some defenses against lions, hyenas, and other predators. Until they are almost three months old, cheetah babies sport a mantle of silvery-gray hair over their backs and heads. Some scientists have speculated that, from a distance, the gray cape makes them resemble a pugnacious mammal called the ratel, a badger-like animal which most predators shun because of its belligerence. As long as cheetah babies can fool predators into thinking, even for a moment, that they are ratels, the cheetahs' chances of survival increase.

An hour later I saw the mother cheetah striding across the plain. Only three cubs followed her now, one limping so badly it could hardly keep up. The life of a cheetah family is a constant hunt for food, yet cheetahs themselves remain always vulnerable to attack.

While adult lions readily team up to attack a buffalo or a giraffe, most adult cheetahs do not cooperate in hunting. When several cheetahs are seen hunting together, they are likely to be all males, perhaps brothers close to adulthood. Even then, the cheetahs never use the coordinated hunting tactics of lions.

And, unlike leopards, cheetahs lack the sheer muscles and power to seize and hold onto larger prey. Because they are not good climbers, cheetahs cannot cache their food in a tree for security, either.

While it does suffer those disadvantages, the cheetah possesses one quality no other cat can match: speed. A creature of the wide-open plains, the cheetah is built for sprinting. Its deep chest houses large lungs and a powerful heart.

But the secret to its speed is the cheetah's supple spine, which coils and uncoils like a spring, catapulting the cat forward. As soon as it has crept close enough to its prey, the cheetah springs out of concealment. Sucking in huge quantities of air, it arches its back and pulls its feet together. Then the spring-like backbone uncurls and the legs shoot out to their fullest extension. As the front legs hit the ground, the spine curls up again, ready to propel the legs out for another push. The flexing and extending of the back adds about 11 percent to the length of the cheetah's total stride, according to biologist Nancy Neff.

In the cheetah, the hind limbs push sequentially rather than together, as in slower animals. Thus for about half the time, a running cheetah has all four feet off the ground at the same time—literally, almost flying. All the while, the long tail streams out behind, a rudder to help the cheetah turn.

The cheetah is the fastest land animal over short distances. When it begins its sprint, the cheetah accelerates in drag-strip fashion, reaching a speed of 70 mph—enough to overtake a gazelle. Yet if the gazelle can twist and turn for just a few minutes, it is safe, for the cheetah cannot maintain its speed.

Say "cheetah" and one response springs to mind—speed. Cheetahs are the world's fastest land animals, clocking a top speed of 70 mph. A cheetah on the run acts like a flexible steel spring, its long legs and supple backbone combining to propel it along in graceful bounds. The cheetah does not have stamina to keep up the pace, however, and must catch prey in the first seconds of a chase.

The dazzling speed provides a tremendous advantage in pursuing fleet hooved animals out in the open. The cheetah needs its speed, since it lacks the long canine teeth which allow other cats to easily bring down large prey.

Unlike most other cats, an adult cheetah cannot retract its claws. Since adult cheetahs do not have fleshy sheaths to cover the claws, the claws are always visible. When the cheetah travels, its claws touch the ground, constantly being dulled, just like those of a dog. Even the pads resemble a dog's: small and tough, with edges that aid in gripping the ground. The pads improve traction for the cheetah, adding to its ability to follow the twists and turns of its prey.

When a cheetah does catch and kill some-

thing, it roughly tears out the entrails and shoves them aside. Dragging a heavy carcass is difficult for the slender cheetah, so it usually eats in the same place it made the kill. A more compelling reason causes the hasty eating, however: if the cheetah doesn't bolt its food, rivals may arrive on the scene to steal its dinner.

The lanky cheetah seems a mix of unusual proportions. It has a small, dome-shaped head, set low, and small rounded ears. Its chest is deep, its waist slender. As in a human sprinter, all surplus weight seems to have been whittled away, leaving only the gaunt outline of a slender, though muscled frame. The cheetah usually weighs less than 130 pounds.

The nostrils are broad, to suck in more

COURSING WITH CHEETAHS

Historically, men of wealth from Egypt to India, such as the Mughal emperor Akbar the Great, used trained cheetahs to hunt deer and other game. When restraining hoods were removed, the swift cat chased down and incapacitated prey, with the master then intervening for collection. Known as coursing, this exotic sport was once popular among European nobility as well.

George Stubbs, 1900s

Young cheetahs get a chance to feed by spreading out in a star formation around freshly-killed prey (below). Unlike other cats, cheetahs seem to disdain rotten meat and thus will seldom return to their kills for a second meal. Young cheetahs (left) are covered with a pale gray fur on their heads and backs for the first few months of life.

oxygen, and the eyes are set high in the head, to better see prey while in tall grass.

Being a daylight hunter, the cheetah has less need for long whiskers to help it pick through dark underbrush. So its whiskers are short and spare.

The cheetah's warm, golden face is set off by two bold, black stripes running from the inner corner of each eye to the mouth. Since the stripes follow the same path a teardrop would, they are called tear stripes. The cub is marked from birth with the same prominent stripes. In the adult, the stripes add a note of distinction, but in the kitten, it seems to mark the fuzzy face with an unexpected frown. Cheetah babies thus seem to carry a permanent scowl.

The cheetah is a relatively shy animal, sensitive to human disruption in its surroundings. This is compounded by its vulnerability to competition and predation by other carnivores. Other carnivores often rob the cheetah of its kills, even until it starves. Being lightly built, a cheetah runs the risk of damage if it tries to fight back. A leopard can survive with a paw missing, but a slight injury to a cheetah's lanky limbs can slow its super-swift pursuit of tomorrow's prey.

A female cheetah purrs loudly while grooming her cub. Unless new conservation measures are quickly put in place, the world may soon lose these elegant members of the cat family. With its habitat being turned into cropland to feed Africa's growing population, the cheetah has become imperiled.

The cheetah's specialized behavior and ecology could make it poorly equipped to adapt to the disruption caused by encroaching human communities. In addition, only a small portion of Africa can be characterized as suitable habitat, such as brushland, open grassland, woodland, and savanna.

For all these reasons, the cheetah is vulnerable to extinction, perhaps more so than some other cats. According to the International Union for Conservation of Nature and Natural Resources (IUCN), about 10,000 to 15,000 cheetahs existed in Africa in mid-1987. A few more are scattered in Iran, the Soviet Union, Saudi Arabia, and Afghanistan, but no one knows exactly how many.

Whatever the number of cheetahs, it is probably only half as many as in 1960. Without new conservation measures, it will surely be cut in half within the next decade.

The cheetah has another, more serious, problem. Scientist Steve O'Brien discovered that cheetahs in South Africa have little genetic variation from one animal to the next. In 1983, he and fellow researchers hypothesized that cheetahs apparently had undergone a drastic near-extinction about 10,000 to 12,000 years ago. The scientists hypothesized that so few cheetahs survived this evolutionary bottleneck that inbreeding soon became inevitable.

If the species lost the genetic variability necessary to adapt to changing environmental conditions, it could more easily be wiped out today. The more variability, the more likely it is that small groups within the total population will carry traits that enable them to survive changed conditions. Since cheetahs seem to be missing gene variability, however, they could be vulnerable.

Can the cheetah withstand all these problems? It has proven resilient in many cases, but if habitat destruction and a uniform gene pool take their toll on the cheetah, this elegant and unusual member of the cat family could soon disappear.

CARACAL
& Other Little-Known Cats

Its pointed ears tipped by tufts of black hair, the caracal (left) looks like a version of the lynx. In earlier times in Iran and India, a few caracals were trained for sport hunting, somewhat as noblemen did with coursing cheetahs. The caracal (right) can literally swat birds on the wing, seizing two or three in a leap.

Pound for pound, the small cats of Africa do not carry as much muscle as a lion or a leopard. But the small cats have made a place for themselves, becoming masters at concealing themselves in the merest bush, even a clump of grass, so they can catch prey.

A small cat does not have massive power to overwhelm its prey, so it depends on quickness and stalking skill. A small cat's slight build usually means that, unlike a big cat, it cannot kill prey large enough to last for several meals. A small cat must generally be content with prey half its size or less, and thus must hunt more often.

Small cats are solitary animals, not inclined to rely on others of their kind to participate in a joint attack to drag down larger prey. This places a premium on surprise and close-quarters attack. A lion or a leopard can sprint for several yards, but a small cat must seize its prey within a stride or two—or be forced to look elsewhere.

For all these reasons, it is inaccurate to say that small cats are "like the big cats, only smaller." They are a whole different story.

While small cats live in some of the same areas as lions, leopards, and cheetahs do, they often favor border zones between two environments—where forest gives way to savanna, for example, or grassland merges into woods. The border zones contain more small prey such as birds, so the small cats can satisfy their own distinctive food needs.

Since they pose no special physical threat to man, small cats do not generate the awe and fear created by the larger, more dangerous beasts. Likewise, the little cats do not enjoy the superstar status of the big cats, so little research money flows in their direction. Small cats have not received much attention from wildlife researchers, and thus our knowledge of them is full of gaps.

These smaller African cats include the wildcat, serval, caracal, golden cat, black-footed cat, and sand cat, which is also found in Asia (see page 113).

CARACAL
Lynx caracal. *Weight: 35-50 lbs.*

The caracal, with its supple body and swift reflexes, is an adept hunter in a broad range of situations. A caracal at work was once recorded by a scientist with a movie camera. He came across the caracal as it was peering at a flock of ground-feeding plovers. When the cat launched its attack from a few yards away, the birds scattered, becoming airborne almost immediately. Still, the caracal caught two of them in a single leap, and the film

The serval's large, rounded ears (opposite) add to its acute sense of hearing. When the serval hears a creature moving (below), it waits for the animal to appear, then quickly grabs it (bottom).

revealed how the cat had changed course in mid-air—somewhat akin to basketball star Michael Jordan going for a dunk.

Both the caracal and the serval show a similar technique for dealing with small prey. With a single sweeping movement they grasp the prey, then fling it a few feet before it can strike back. While the surprised creature is recovering, they pounce on it again, only to repeat the entire routine. After several such attacks, which leave the prey thoroughly battered, the cat carries through a final assault. It grips the prey with teeth and claws, until the last struggle fades away.

A recent study in South Africa showed that caracals do not always toy with their victims, however. Whether they do or not depends on the prey's size.

The caracal is a powerful medium-sized cat and can kill an animal twice its size, such as the male mountain reedbuck, which can weigh nearly 70 pounds. The caracal is essentially an animal of dry areas, and its nickname is "desert lynx."

SERVAL
Felis serval. *Weight: Males, 22-39 lbs. Females, 19-27 lbs.*

In proportion to the rest of its body, the serval has the longest legs in the cat kingdom. The long legs help the serval peer over tall vegetation to find prey.

The serval also depends on some highly-tuned hearing apparatus. The serval's large, oval ears, looking a tad ludicrous atop the slight body, help this agile small cat survive in several million square miles of Africa, along the water courses in grasslands, woodlands, and thickets.

The serval tries not to show itself and moves with extreme care, in keeping with its life as a solitary medium-sized cat.

The serval is not all that powerful, but it *is* quick. Suspecting a rodent in a patch of grass, the serval will leap to and fro until the frightened rodent scampers from its cover. Once something stirs, the serval's reflexes

Like its faraway relative, the Asian golden cat, the African golden cat can be grey or red or even spotted.

are usually quick enough to grab it.

Although the serval weighs no more than 35 pounds and is delicate in build, it can take birds as large as a guineafowl, weighing perhaps 10 pounds. Sometimes it tackles hares or duikers, but does not ignore lizards and fish. The serval's prey generally amounts to small rodents and ground birds.

The serval sometimes hunts in the early morning hours and late afternoon. During the hot hours of midday, it prefers to rest in an abandoned aardvark burrow, or under a shady bush. At night, it often hunts again.

A good place to spot a serval is in the moorlands of Aberdare National Park. Even through the mist and fog, you can sight it with only a fair degree of luck and a good pair of eyes. In Kenya, it lives in the hot coastal belt, in the thornscrub of Tsava Park, in savanna woodlands, and in mountain areas.

Its color is yellowish with black spots, but it often appears in melanistic or darkened

form, as do other cats living in moist conditions above 10,000 feet.

The serval is blessed with fine markings on its fur, but unfortunately that makes it a prime target of poachers. Populations of servals in the wild may sustain this exploitation for a few years. On the other hand, widespread pressure could greatly depress the number of servals.

GOLDEN CAT
Felis aurata. *Weight: 11-35 lbs.*

The golden cat leads such a discreet life in the African forests that a den with young has yet to be reported. This fact, along with the cat's short legs, has prompted some scientists to claim an arboreal lifestyle for this cat.

Separated by thousands of miles from its close relative, the Asian golden cat, the African golden cat varies from golden brown to dark grey. Patterns vary from cat to cat.

It inhabits forests of the west African coast from Sierra Leone to Cameroon, Uganda, Zaire, and Kenya. Hand-reared cats are reported to be loving pets, but the captured wild adult is said to be quite ferocious.

BLACK-FOOTED CAT
Felis nigripes. *Average weight: 4 lbs.*

This tiny felid, one of the world's smallest cat species, averages four pounds and may grow to be all of 18 inches long.

A solitary lifestyle makes ecological sense for these little cats. If two or more of these tiny carnivores hunted together for any length of time, the food source might quickly disappear. Thus the black-footed cat is probably a solitary hunter, eating everything from lizards and beetles to elephant shrews. The black-footed cat goes about at twilight or at night and rests during the day in old termite mounds or the former burrows of springhares and other animals.

The young cats display an interesting response to threats. When their mother calls an alarm, they scatter and freeze until they hear her give a distinctive all-clear signal.

The black-footed cat is found in dry country. The hair on its feet likely protects it from hot sand, and its large auditory vesicles help it find subterranean beetles.

The pads of its feet usually are black, giving the cat its name.

AFRICAN WILDCAT
Felis silvestris. *Weight: 11-35 lbs.*

The African wildcat is an ancestor of the domestic cat (see page 176). Like other felids, it eats small rodents and birds as large as hens, with insects and lizards thrown in for good measure. Like some other cats, the wildcat sometimes seems to need plenty of fresh grass in its diet to keep in good condition. The African wildcat is the same animal as the European forest wildcat (see page 120).

Neither the feisty wildcat nor any of its small felid relatives cause much aggravation for stockmen. They are also far more adaptable to man than other wild cats are. Because of their different diets, small cats also are more adaptive to changes in their habitats. Since small cats live off birds, rodents, and even lizards and snakes, the decline of larger prey animals will not directly affect them.

"Our knowledge of the cats of Africa is directly proportional to their size," noted naturalist Armand Denis. He was writing in 1964, but it is just as true today. This black-footed cat, among the smallest of feline species, is one of many needing to be studied in the wild.

African wildcats (right) thrive in scrub, bush, and savanna, but also prowl the byways of nearby communities, where they often breed with domestic cats. African wildcats are the likely ancestors of our domestic cats.

A bird-hunting cat accompanies its nobleman master in this detail of an Egyptian wall painting from 3,500 years ago.

The Egyptians had a special reverence for felines. Their goddess of joy and love, Bastet (above), was depicted as a cat. Archeologists have discovered the remains of thousands of mummified cats, such as the one at right.

In fact when cornfields replace grasslands and when rain forests are chopped down, the resulting forms of vegetation may actually supply better conditions for rats, seed-eating birds, and the other small creatures that make up the diet of small cats.

All these facts combined may someday signal a growing population of small cats.

THE CAT'S ALLIANCE WITH HUMANS

Our household cat is a domesticated descendant of the African wildcat. That much we think we know. We don't know how the process occurred, when it first happened, or why the first wild cat was coaxed into becoming a companion of humans.

So far as we can discern, the ancient Egyptians first featured *Felis catus* as a member of their entourage of domesticated animals—and it was not as a pet or rat catcher, but as a religious entity. Cats appear in Egyptian records as sacred creatures from 1600 B.C. onward. Because of their religious significance, large numbers of cats were mummified and buried.

This phenomenon was illustrated at the start of this century, when nineteen tons of cat remains were unearthed in Egypt and sent to Britain to be used as fertilizer. Only a single skull was retained for examination to determine the ancestry of the creature.

Fortunately a later excavation of tombs at Gizeh turned up 190 cat skulls, dating from 600-200 B.C., and the domestic cat's pedigree was better established as deriving from the African wildcat.

We know from Egyptian paintings that their cats were generally ginger in color, with dark markings on their ears and forelimbs, and with a dark-ringed tail. Since our modern cats feature colors other than ginger, we can surmise some breeding has taken place with the European wildcat, a sub-species. Beyond that, our knowledge is scant indeed.

OUR LIVES

BY ELAINE S. FURLOW

CATS AND CULTURE

Cat fascination hit Broadway in the 1982 musical "Cats." Actors caricatured cats through imaginative costumes (left), movement, and music. Along the Peru-Brazil border, a girl of the Mayoruna tribe (right) adorns herself in imitation of her tribe's totem animal, the cougar. She wears whiskers of palm tree spines and a tattoo around her mouth.

Wild cats have been seen by Indian tribes as powerful totems. In modern times, one of the most popular circus acts in the United States is still a tiger act—Gunther Gebel-Williams and his trained big cats. On any fall weekend, countless teen-age Tigers face off against a like number of fierce Wildcats on football fields across the United States. In the movies, MGM is still known worldwide by its lion logo. And Liz Taylor says that, given the choice in a new life, she might like to come back as "one of the jungle cats."

Our culture is interwoven with the influence of many animals, but perhaps no creature has found its way into our lives as often as the cat. Now domestic cats even seem to have overtaken dogs as the number one pet in the United States. More than 56 million cats live in American households, compared to about 52 million dogs.

Wild cats—not always popular with settlers, farmers, and ranchers—have sometimes had a struggle to maintain their niche in the world. But now even the wild ones seem to have won new admiration from humans, and a few of the once-feared wild cats are beginning to make a comeback.

What is it about cats, wild and domestic, that attracts modern-day humans? Unlike dogs, domestic cats seldom seem overeager to please. One writer summed it up nicely: "If I tell my dog, 'Come here,' he runs right over with a 'Yes, what can I do for you?' look. The cat's response is, 'Put it in writing and I'll get back to you.'"

Perhaps it is that touch of aloofness, a bit of independent wildness in the animal, that attracts us. Perhaps it is just the creature's grace and style. We humans admire wild cats for some of the same reasons we enjoy our tame domestic ones: their amusing antics, their independent nature, their sleek maneuvering, their mix of stealth and shyness.

For whatever reason, the cats of the world enthrall us, chill us, delight us; from the self-confident stalking of the tiger to the

lithe, leaping moves of the margay; from the cheetah pungently marking its home range to the domestic cat entreatingly rubbing against our legs. The wild cats are, after all, similar to our domestic cats in many physical respects. They just happen to live in the wild.

But no domestic cat could scare us the way the big wild ones do. All wild cats are superbly equipped, patient and powerful, for the business of taking prey. For the big cat the taut muscles and bounding movement can coalesce in one fluid moment to bring down a deer, a zebra, and yes, rarely, a human being. It's not surprising that many American Indians and travelers took special note when they spotted wild cats about.

Writing about Florida in 1598, explorer Rene Laudonniere reported having observed "a certain kind of beast that differeth little from the lyon of Africa." In 1610, Captain John Smith reported that "there be in this country lions, beares, woulves." Settlers in New York agreeably bought the cougar skins that Indians brought to trade, but wondered

Early hunters such as this man in Beaumont, Texas (above) collected bounties for dead bobcats. By the 1980s, however, virtually all bounties had been dropped. The fashion industry also took its toll on cats. A snow leopard coat (left) was featured in the National Fur Fashion parade in London. A 1975 international law (CITES) made it illegal to trade in the skins of endangered species.

why the skins were of "maneless lions" only. "The males live among the mountains many days' travel away, and are so fierce that nobody in his right mind would dare go after them," the Indians replied.

In the 1800s, anxious pioneers reported cougars attacking livestock and sometimes even humans. Bounties for dead bobcats and cougars were common, and the hunting of them was widespread.

Myths grew up around the cougar's terrifying strength, and outdoorsmen of all stripes traded stories about the cougar's scream. The early vision of wild cats was shaped, in part, by particular needs and fears. The cattleman who felt threatened by the cougar was in no mood to hear about its majesty; the hunter who tracked it felt he was after an elusive and worthy prey.

The cougar, or "painter" as it was called in some parts, thus became fair game for many a hunter. James Whitcomb Riley captured the image when he wrote:

> Yes—and painters, *prowlin' 'bout,*
> *Allus darkest nights.—Lay out*
> *Clost yer cattle.—Great, big red*
> *Eyes a-blazin' in their head,*
> *Glitter'n' 'long the timber-line—*
> *Shine out some, and then* un-shine,
> *And shine back—Then stiddy!*
> *Whizz!*
> *'N' there yer Mr. Painter is*
> *With a hole bored spang between*
> *Them-air eyes!*

The hunting of big cats became an enduring part of American literature and legend. In his story "Cougar-Catching on the Siwash," Zane Grey recounted the adventures of one Buffalo Jones, who caught his cougars the hard way—by lasso. Even luminaries such as Teddy Roosevelt hunted cougars, but had a hard time even finding them without the help of hunting dogs.

Roosevelt saw a live cougar only twice.

"Beside a recently travelled game trail," he wrote in 1893, "I lay quiet for about an hour, listening to the murmur of the pine forests and the call of a jay or woodpecker. . . . Suddenly, without noise or warning of any kind, a cougar stood in the trail before me. The unlooked for and unheralded approach of the beast was fairly ghost-like. With its head lower than its shoulders, and its long tail twitching, it slouched down the path, treading as softly as a kitten."

The mystery of the cat, be it cougar in America or cheetah in Africa, helped to contribute to man's awe or fear. Those feelings were woven into folklore, fashion, literature, and art. Scanning the world's cultures, we find the cat used over and over again as a symbol. Sometimes it is a symbol of mystery, sometimes a reminder of power.

In England, the red and gold image of a lion on his flag followed Richard the Lionhearted into battle. Centuries later, Haile Selassie, the redoubtable emperor of Ethiopia from the 1940s to the 1960s, bore the title "Lion of Judah."

Jaguar images have appeared throughout Latin America on massive temples and on handwoven shirts. In the Buddhist religion, one of Buddha's disciples is depicted riding a huge tiger, thus exhibiting his supernatural powers and ability to overcome "evil."

American culture and tradition, in particular, are peppered with memories of the wild cat. Go-getters in Oklahoma and Texas took their chances on "wildcat" oil wells, so-called because success was in doubt.

The term "wildcatter" may have different origins in different settings, but in the banking field, its history is documented through a tattered $5 note from the Catskill Bank in New York in the 1800s. On the note is a drawing of a cougar, often seen then in the region. With a number of the notes in circulation, the bank proceeded to go under, and other banks whose solvency was in question came to be called "wildcat banks."

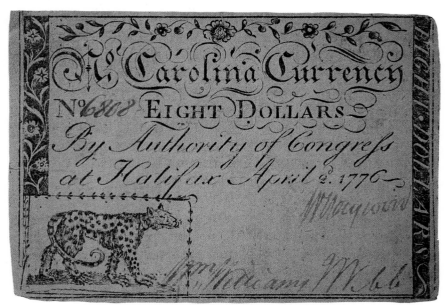

The term "wildcatter," meaning a person who undertakes a risky venture, may have originated with a mid-1800s bank whose currency featured a cougar (top). When the bank failed, the "wildcat" notes were worthless. Cats also decorated a North Carolina note (above) in 1776, Delaware money (left) in 1759, and a commemorative coin from the 1927 Vermont sesquicentennial.

In The Wizard of Oz, actor Bert Lahr played the cowardly lion (right) in a classic performance. In 1924 the Metro-Goldwyn-Mayer film company adopted its roaring lion trademark, now familiar to millions (below, right). Patience and Fortitude, stone lions in front of the New York Public Library, have impassively greeted patrons through the years. For the library's 75th anniversary, the lions (only one is shown below) sported top hats and ties.

75
A BUILDING TO CELEBRATE
The New York Public Library
1911 – 1986

ARS GRATIA ARTIS
TRADE   MARK
Metro Goldwyn Mayer

Meanwhile in New York, the marble lions Patience and Fortitude had been installed in front of the New York Public Library. Put in place in 1911, the two were not well received, at least at first. Some people thought an elk or moose would have been more appropriate; others preferred the industrious beaver. But since then the lions have become a popular landmark. In the spring, garlands are draped around their necks, and at Christmas, they wear evergreen wreaths and red bows.

In World War II, a group of American volunteers provided aerial support for the Burma Road, a vital supply line from India. Led by Gen. Claire Lee Chennault, they nicknamed themselves the Flying Tigers, and became one of the best-known and most effective American units of World War II.

Through the years, hundreds of American schools adopted wild cat names and mascots for their athletic teams, from Penn State's mighty Nittany Lions to the Dimmitt High School Bobcats in west Texas.

Of course, the Nittany lion doesn't appear in any taxonomy systems. It became Penn State's athletic symbol in 1904, after Penn State students refused to be impressed with the tiger of their rival, Princeton, and proclaimed their own Nittany lion to be "the fiercest beast of all." They were referring to the cougar, which had roamed the Nittany valley near the school decades earlier.

Down at Louisiana State, students in 1936 chipped in to buy a Bengal tiger mascot, nicknamed Mike after the team's trainer. In her book *The Animals' Who's Who,* Ruthven Tremain relates this anecdote: A later mascot named Mike III became so popular that when he was injured in a highway accident, dozens of people offered to donate blood.

And the Metro-Goldwyn-Mayer movie company used a lion as its symbol, complete with roar, to open films. After a while, the company switched to a modern logo using a stylized lion. In the 1980s, however, a live, full-maned lion returned to play the part.

In *The Wonderful Wizard of Oz,* L. Frank Baum's classic, the cowardly lion joined the expedition to the Emerald City in the hope that the Wizard would give him courage. The 1939 movie featured actor Bert Lahr as the lion, lumbering around in a bulky lion suit, while a stagehand managed the awkward tail with a fishing rod.

In the 1960s, Americans lined up at the box office to see *Born Free,* the movie about Elsa, an orphaned lioness raised by George and Joy Adamson in Kenya. And later the stage musical "Cats " was a box office hit across the United States.

A tiger turned into an advertising legend for an American oil company. After World War II, a tiger was used to advertise Esso's gasoline. "Other campaigns came along, but every time we tried to drop the tiger, we had to bring it back again at the request of . . . the retail trade," recalled Bernard Allen, then advertising manager, in a company history.

"Now remember—roar just as you leap. . . . These things have some of the greatest expressions."

Bizarre and hilarious comments on life from the imagined perspective of animals—that's the trademark of cartoonist Gary Larson's series titled The Far Side. *In a 1987 show, the Smithsonian Institution in Washington, D.C., featured Larson's animal cartoons.*

Consumers worldwide were urged to "Put a tiger in your tank" by buying Esso (forerunner of Exxon) gasoline in the 1950s (right). Car makers, too, capitalized on the power conveyed by images of cats. Jaguar, Peugeot, and Lincoln-Mercury (below) all have featured cats in their logos.

Emery Smyth, a young Chicago copywriter, added the tagline urging motorists to "put a tiger in your tank," and the ad appeared in 1959 over the trademark of the Humble Oil Company (a sister company to Esso, and a forerunner of today's Exxon). The slogan caught on immediately. Research showed that people easily understood that "power" was the commercials' main idea.

Today, Americans seem enamored of cats, both domestic and wild. When in 1986 several famous Americans were asked what animal they would like to be, a goodly number chose felines. In Fleur Cowles' book *If I Were an Animal*, author Jackie Collins revealed, "I believe strongly in reincarnation, and I have no doubt that my return to earth will be as a leopard. My house in California is full of paintings, bronzes and china ornaments of leopards. Once, a long time ago, someone gave me a leopard coat. Every time I wore it I got the strangest feeling and found I couldn't wear it comfortably."

A Minnesota hotel, striving to provide a homey touch, keeps fifteen cuddly housecats on call. Guests can adopt a cat for the evening. At last report, all fifteen were being spoken for every night.

Cats have been inspiration for movies, stories, and songs. In the folk song "South Coast," the Kingston Trio poured forth the lament of a lonely man who lived in cougar territory decades ago. "The south coast, the wild coast is lonely," they sang . . . "the lion still rules the Barranca, and a man there is always alone." Barranca is a Spanish word for a cliff or ravine, and many mountain lions, or cougars, roamed those rugged hills.

Country artist Buck Owens belted out "I've Got a Tiger by the Tail, It's Plain to See," and Survivor's "Eye of the Tiger," the theme song from the movie *Rocky III*, was number one on the charts for weeks.

Artists worldwide have found inspiration in cats for countless paintings, sculptures, and designs. Henri Rousseau, who greatly

influenced primitive art, created vivid jungle paintings in the late 1800s. Rousseau's bold colors most often featured lions and tigers in fanciful settings.

While Rousseau's cats were never very true to life, other artists took a different approach. Canadian naturalist and wildlife artist Robert Bateman does extensive field work and insists on knowing his subjects intimately before he paints them. "I try to portray an animal living its own life independent from man," he says. "Sometimes I try to hold my face in the expression of the animal I'm painting. I feel I am getting into its skin and this helps me get a good likeness."

The realistic paintings of Guy Coheleach seem to capture the wild cats' amazing changeability—the ripple of muscles, the glint in an eye, the roar, the burst of speed. The cats' movements almost transcend the canvas on which he created them.

And such a wealth of movements, as well as ways to convey them. A Japanese artist who once painted the tiger was criticized by a westerner, who said his tiger was anatomically incorrect. "Yes, possibly," the artist replied, "but morally, it is perfect."

If pen and brush help capture the magic and mystery of the world's cats, so, too, do well-chosen words. Poet Ted Hughes describes the purposeful gait of a jaguar:

> *Skinful of bowls, he bowls them,*
> *The hip going in and out of joint,*
> *dropping the spine*
> *With the urgency of his hurry*

How to portray the sinuous movement of a cat? Carl Sandburg coined a classic line when he described fog that "comes in on cat feet." And every owner of a pet cat could delight in Rosalie Moore's apt characterization in her poem "Catalog":

> *Cats sleep fat and walk thin.*
> *Cats, when they sleep, slump;*
> *When they wake, stretch and begin*
> *over, pulling their ribs in.*
> *Cats walk thin.*

Portraying the cat in words and art is nothing new, of course. Our Stone Age ancestors, fascinated by the big cats, depicted them on cave walls. Later people incorporated them in carvings, headdresses, and crafts. An American Indian beaded bag (see page 34), for instance, shows the Underwater Panther, a fearsome mythical beast which could pull down into its lair a fishermen who happened its way, using its awesome power to control the water and storms. Indians thus feared and revered it.

Early Latin American people looked upon the jaguar as a powerful totem. In ancient Mexico and Guatemala, Indians laboriously constructed temples to pay homage to the powerful cat. In Peru, natives fashioned

While some Americans suffer from ailurophobia (an abnormal fear of cats), the majority seem to love felines, in whatever form. The NCAA handbook lists 33 college athletic teams who have adopted feisty cougars, tigers, wildcats, leopards, or lions as their mascots. Louisiana State (above) and Clemson (left) both claim the tiger. Cartoon cats such as Jim Davis' Garfield (top), here imitating a tiger, are well-known in comic strips, books, calendars, and even on bed sheets.

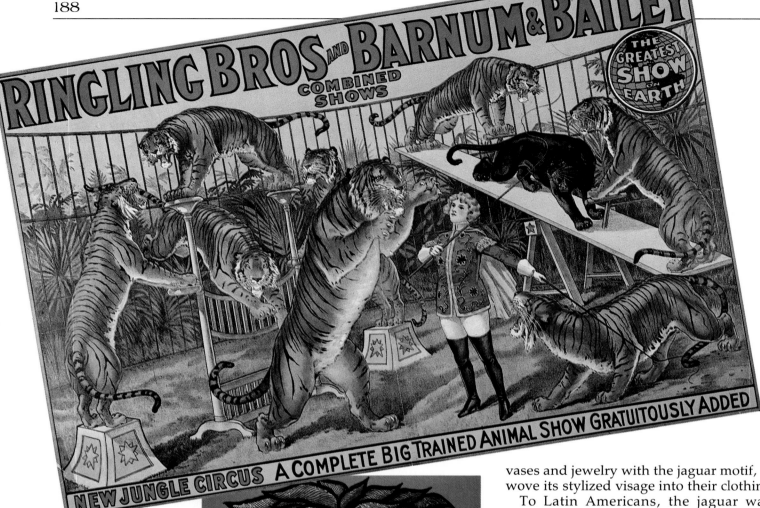

If one needs testimony to the international appeal of big cats on display, try this 1920s circus poster from the United States (above) or one from Poland in 1967 (right).

vases and jewelry with the jaguar motif, and wove its stylized visage into their clothing.

To Latin Americans, the jaguar was a predator, true, but also a powerful god and protector. If they could somehow get on the jaguar's good side, they reasoned, it might guarantee their safety and good health. Cat gods of one kind or another were revered from Mexico to Chile.

Not every use of the cat was benevolent, of course. Powerful tribal medicine men practiced rituals, believing themselves to be creatures with some of the characteristics of cats, and some of men. In Africa, mystical cults sprang up around these were-leopards and were-lions. Similar ceremonies were performed in Asia with were-tigers, and in Latin America with were-jaguars.

And worldwide, big cats were hunted for their fur, fangs, and other body parts. In the 1960s, fashion-conscious women fueled a demand for furs that continued unabated until controls such as CITES (Convention on International Trade in Endangered Species, Flora and Fauna) were put in place in the mid-1970s.

Despite some success stories of protecting

wild cats, the market for their pelts and body parts is still marked by poaching and smuggling. For tigers, one demand may derive from traditional oriental medicinal uses: the tail (for skin ointment), whiskers (for a charm for courage), penis (for an aphrodisiac), ground bone (for headaches). Cat furs and products make up a sizeable proportion of all illegal wildlife seized from tourists returning to the United States.

Most visitors, thankfully, are content to return home with photographs and memories. Many a tourist to Africa might consider the trip unsuccessful if he doesn't see lions, leopards, and cheetahs. If he can't get to Africa, however, then he might get a glimpse of the cats through literature and art, zoos, and circuses.

No one claims circuses mirror the real life of cats in the wild, but we can still marvel at performers such as Gunther Gebel-Williams and his circus troupe of tigers.

Long before the Christian era in Rome, the displaying of wild beasts was already an art form in Egypt. A procession put together by Ptolemy II, for example, included camels loaded high with spices and perfumes, 24 enormous lions, a choir of 600 men, 2,000 bulls wearing gold, exotic birds in cages, and on and on. The procession started at dawn and took all day to pass through the stadium.

Later the Romans put on colossal, often gruesome spectacles, such as the lions versus the Christians.

Toward the end of the eighteenth century, the modern circus got its start in London. Philip Astley, an enterprising showman, put together trained animals, tightrope walkers, clowns, and jugglers in a show that attracted hundreds of delighted onlookers. It didn't take long for this new creation to cross the Atlantic to America.

At the end of the nineteenth century, Americans sang about a man who "sticks his head in the lion's mouth and leaves it there a while; and when he takes it out again, he

With a leopard casually draped across his shoulders, trainer Gunther Gebel-Williams enthralls another crowd. He and his famous troupe have entertained thousands of people.

greets you with a smile." They were talking about Isaac A. Van Amburgh, one of the world's greatest lion-trainers.

Legend has it that at 19, when Van Amburgh was reading the biblical account of Daniel in the lions' den, he decided to become a lion-tamer. He first experimented at the Bronx Zoo in New York, when he confronted several fearsome animals and controlled them with ease.

Among the most enduring of all trainers was Mabel Stark, a slender blonde who bedeviled the manager of the Al G. Barnes show to give her a chance at tiger-training. Finally she was permitted to try out with three tigers. She emerged alive and unharmed. From there she progressed to an act in which sixteen tigers obeyed her will, at least most of the time.

In 1928, Stark was performing in a ring slippery from rain, and the animals were tense. Sheik, a tiger she had refused to eliminate even though he was said to be a killer, sneaked up on Stark when she slipped in the mud. In a gruesome scene, he ripped at her left leg. Two months and many stitches later, Stark was back in the ring, performing as she always had. Such experiences show that while cats may be trained, they are not tame.

The excitement of unexpected danger is one of the attractions of the circus, and of wild cats in particular. For most folks, the circus conjures up the image of an adventurous world beyond the boundaries of everyday lives, similar, perhaps, to that felt by the people of long ago who made their way to the slopes overlooking the Roman Circus Maximus. Now, from Moscow, Berlin, and Stockholm come headline acts that draw modern-day patrons to the big top.

City-dwellers can enjoy another glimpse of how wild cats live by going to zoos, especially ones which feature open habitats. Snow leopards roam with easy grace through a section of the Bronx Zoo (New York), while cougars prowl near-natural environs at the new, $2.5 million "Mountain Habitat" at the Arizona-Sonora Desert Museum (Tucson).

A half million people a year walk within inches of the two cougars there in a simulated woodland mountain habitat. The rocks are artificial, but everything else—vegetation, organisms, predators—are those one would find naturally occuring in Arizona or Sonora, Mexico. "The [cougar] exhibit in particular gives the impression of a steep rock wall," says Peter Siminski, curator of birds and mammals. "We have hardy junipers, live oak, and then the mountain lions. That's just the way you'd find it if you were in the area, except the mountain lion is a solitary animal and you wouldn't see it. Here you can."

At the Bronx Zoo, visitors to the Himalayan Highlands exhibit can look for six snow leopards in a rocky setting, complete with a stream, that approximates the cats' natural habitat in Asia. Scree slopes that face east were chosen so the big cats could keep cool. Behind one hill is an area for the snow leopards in the zoo's captive breeding program; two litters were born there in 1987.

Before the exhibit opened in 1986, the snow leopards had been in typical cages. "Nothing bad about that," says Jim Doherty, general curator, "but that is not reality." The new exhibit comes closer to reality, leaving one with the impression of being on a cool Asian mountainside—despite the fact that the zoo is surrounded by the concrete canyons of New York City.

It's not quite the same as catching sight of a snow leopard in the mountain wilds of Asia, of course, but then even experienced researchers who have spent years studying the big cats have had trouble doing that. Yet such glimpses into the lives of wild cats help to answer our curiosity: What are the wild cats like? What is it that draws us to them? It lets us appreciate those qualities that have engendered such human admiration and fear through the years, and encourages us to save a place in our lives for the cats of the world.

Leopard by Robert Bateman

Lynx by Manfred Schatz

Many well-known wildlife artists have captured on canvas the mystique of the world's wild cats.

Overleaf: *Cheetah chasing Thomson's gazelle by Guy Coheleach*

Snow leopard by Ed Bierly

A PLACE FOR CATS

How many species of cats might we lose before the end of this century? If habitat loss and illegal trade continue, several species such as this leopard could vanish. Why worry about saving cats? Because their beauty, power, and grace fill a particular aesthetic and ecological niche in the natural world. Wiping out a species leaves a void and permanently alters the ecosystem.

The lynx was wiped out in much of central Europe in the 1800s. No trace of the Caspian tiger has been found for decades. In 1952, the Indian cheetah was declared extinct. No one has seen a jaguar in the wild in the United States since 1971.

The list is a depressing litany, and it could go on. Thirty-seven species of wild cats remain, but some may vanish within the next 20 years, just as people worldwide are beginning to appreciate their full value.

Cats are endangered because growing human settlements wipe out their habitats. The disappearance of prey deprives cats of their normal food source, and that brings them into conflict with humans and their livestock, leading inevitably to the reprisal killing of cats. Moreover, cats have long been hunted, sometimes for sport, sometimes because they are competitors for prey, and often for their pelts and body parts.

All these reasons have combined to make several species of cats vulnerable to extinction.* Some scientists also fear that not enough genetic diversity is present in small populations. That reduces the cats' long-term ability to adapt to natural changes in their environment.

Though human activities are largely responsible for the deteriorating status of cats, human activities can also change it. The cat specialist group of the International Union for Conservation of Nature and Natural Resources (IUCN) has come up with a strategy, and first on the list is protecting habitat.

Any American who has seen fields and forests give way to shopping centers and subdivisions knows how rapidly habitat can change. What is not so evident, at least to a layman's eye, is the ripple effect on animals

In 1987, fifteen feline species and several sub-species or specific populations were listed on Appendix I of CITES, which means they are in danger of extinction. The remainder of the cat family is on Appendix II, meaning they are threatened or may become so unless trade is carefully regulated.

In the 1970s, Maurice Hornocker (right) and his assistants put radio collars on cougars, then tracked them to obtain details on territory and habits. Perched atop an elephant, biologist John Seidensticker (below) prepares a drug to subdue tigers for study during a research project in India.

and plants. When a cat's habitat is taken away, it forever alters that cat's way of life —what prey it has available and how hard the cat must work to catch it, and how easily the cat can mate and raise young.

"Whether we're talking about the Amazon or Africa, preserving habitat is a priority," says S. Douglas Miller, National Wildlife Federation vice president. Several years ago, staff members of the Federation's International Division pressed the World Bank to consider the effect on natural resources, including habitat, when making loans to Third World countries. "If building a dam is going to damage habitat, then the World Bank should require mitigation before it makes the loan," Federation officials reasoned. The bank recently agreed to establish an environmental department to handle just such issues. Negotiations also are underway to get

the World Bank and other international government lenders to collaborate more closely with Third World conservation groups.

Making people aware of habitat loss and other problems is a never-ending task, with different approaches for different problems.

The Federation has sponsored two international cat symposia. The first, in Front Royal, Va., in 1978, focused on the bobcat. The second, in 1981, brought a diverse mix of scientists, resource managers, researchers, and agency officials to Kingsville, Texas.

Because of the Federation's efforts, a computerized data base has been initiated to monitor all cat research. Dozens of researchers are out there in the jungles and mountains, tracking cats and recording data. NWF officials hope the data base, which will be operational in 1988, will allow a researcher to punch in questions about a kodkod, for instance, to find out what work has been done and what is underway.

In wildlife management, money is never abundant enough to study and manage all species, so the crisis situations tend to get the attention. Still, the Federation hopes to improve wildlife management to conserve certain species. Also, training customs agents to better recognize regulated species hopefully will increase compliance with trade laws such as CITES (Convention of International Trade in Endangered Species of Wild Fauna and Flora). CITES now has been signed by 95 countries, yet could be strengthened by adding penalties or incentives for compliance.

In addition to saving habitat and enforcing trade laws, we can help cats by knowing more about them. Detailed information is needed about distribution, numbers, and habitat. "We are probably never going to get a good census technique for cats," Miller points out, "because of the nature of cats, and their wide range. Reliable figures from research could detect changes in cat populations, but exactly how sensitive an indicator do we need? Should scientists be able

Domestic kittens born through in vitro *(test tube) fertilization in 1987 were the world's first (left). The technique may someday be one of many solutions to help conserve endangered species. Stopping the trade in cat skins may also help. U.S. Fish and Wildlife officials (below) are still confiscating illegally imported cat skins. In the past, ocelot, jaguar and tiger skins seemed to make up most seized shipments. Today, the pelts of small felines such as Geoffroy's cat appear more often.*

to detect a 1 percent change, a 5 percent change, or just a 25 percent change?"

Many such challenges await researchers, but many achievements already are behind them, too. In April, 1987, the National Zoo in Washington, D.C. reported the first successful birth of domestic kittens by *in vitro* (test tube) fertilization. The achievement was heralded because it is often difficult to get captive cats to breed. The pioneering work holds promise for increasing the long-term survival prospects of endangered species such as Pallas' cat.

Research on gene pools and breeding is just one of many avenues that need to be explored. "Personally," says Miller, "I'd like to change people, not biology. I wouldn't want people thinking that it's okay if cats or their habitat are gone, assuming we can just make another tiger out of a frozen embyro."

Saving species of cats is a task to which the Federation, along with many other groups, is committed. Even desperate situations can be reversed if we know enough, plan well enough, and act vigorously enough.

The Bengal tiger had declined to dangerously low levels by 1970, but a dedicated group of conservationists in India and Nepal, bolstered by international support, helped it recover. The battle isn't won yet, but at least the tiger may be on the upswing. The same can happen for cheetahs, Florida panthers, and many other species and sub-species that today stand on the brink. Thousands of people worldwide share the conviction that we shall not see the wild cats disappear from the earth in our time.

Tomorrow holds promise for preserving all species of cats—if wildlife managers, concerned citizens, and legislators act decisively today.

INDEX

CREDITS

WRITERS

Fiona Sunquist
is a roving editor for *National* and *International Wildlife*. In 1987, she wrote *Tiger Moon*, a book on tigers. Her work has appeared in *Smithsonian*, National Geographic *World*, and other publications.

Gary Turbak
is a freelance writer and cat lover. His work has appeared in *National* and *International Wildlife, Reader's Digest,* and numerous other magazines. His latest book is *America's Great Cats*, published in 1986 by Northland Press.

Peter Jackson
is chairman of the cat specialist group of the Species Survival Commission, International Union for Conservation of Nature and Natural Resources (IUCN). He became fascinated by wildlife, and especially tigers, during nearly twenty years as a foreign correspondent in India. He was project officer of the World Wildlife Fund's Operation Tiger, until becoming a freelance writer and consultant in 1979.

Norman Myers
studied lions, cheetahs, leopards, and small cats during his 24 years in Africa. Myers now lives in England, where he pursues his writing and research career. He is a roving editor of *National* and *International Wildlife.*

Elaine S. Furlow
is senior book editor for the National Wildlife Federation. She previously worked on Capitol Hill, in the Carter White House, and as a book editor in Atlanta.

NATIONAL WILDLIFE FEDERATION
1412 Sixteenth St., N.W., Washington, D.C. 20036-2266